I0817477

CONTEMPORARY SOUTHERN *Vernacular*

CONTEMPORARY SOUTHERN *Vernacular*

Creating Sustainable Houses for Hot, Humid Climates

JANE & MICHAEL FREDERICK

4880 Lower Valley Road • Atglen, PA 19310

Other Schiffer Books on Related Subjects:
Contemporary Southern Homes, E. Ashley Rooney, 978-0-7643-4682-8
Designing for Disaster: Domestic Architecture in the Era of Climate Change, Boyce Thompson, 978-0-7643-5784-8

Library of Congress Control Number: 2025930109

Design by Neeley Spotts
Cover design by Molly Shields
All sketches by Michael Frederick
Type set in Omnes/Gentium Plus

Ends image: Reed white roof perspective background. White ceiling beams pattern background. Architecture and construction concept. Full frame. © Su NITRAM, Courtesy of Bigstock.

ISBN: 978-0-7643-6982-7
ePub: 978-1-5073-0599-7

Printed in China

10 9 8 7 6 5 4 3 2 1

Published by Schiffer Publishing, Ltd.
4880 Lower Valley Road
Atglen, PA 19310
Phone: (610) 593-1777; Fax: (610) 593-2002
Email: info@schifferbooks.com
Web: www.schifferbooks.com

To our grandchildren,
Charlotte, Norah, Fred, Zöe, and Sara Jane,
because later is too late

Courtesy of Helen Norman

CONTENTS

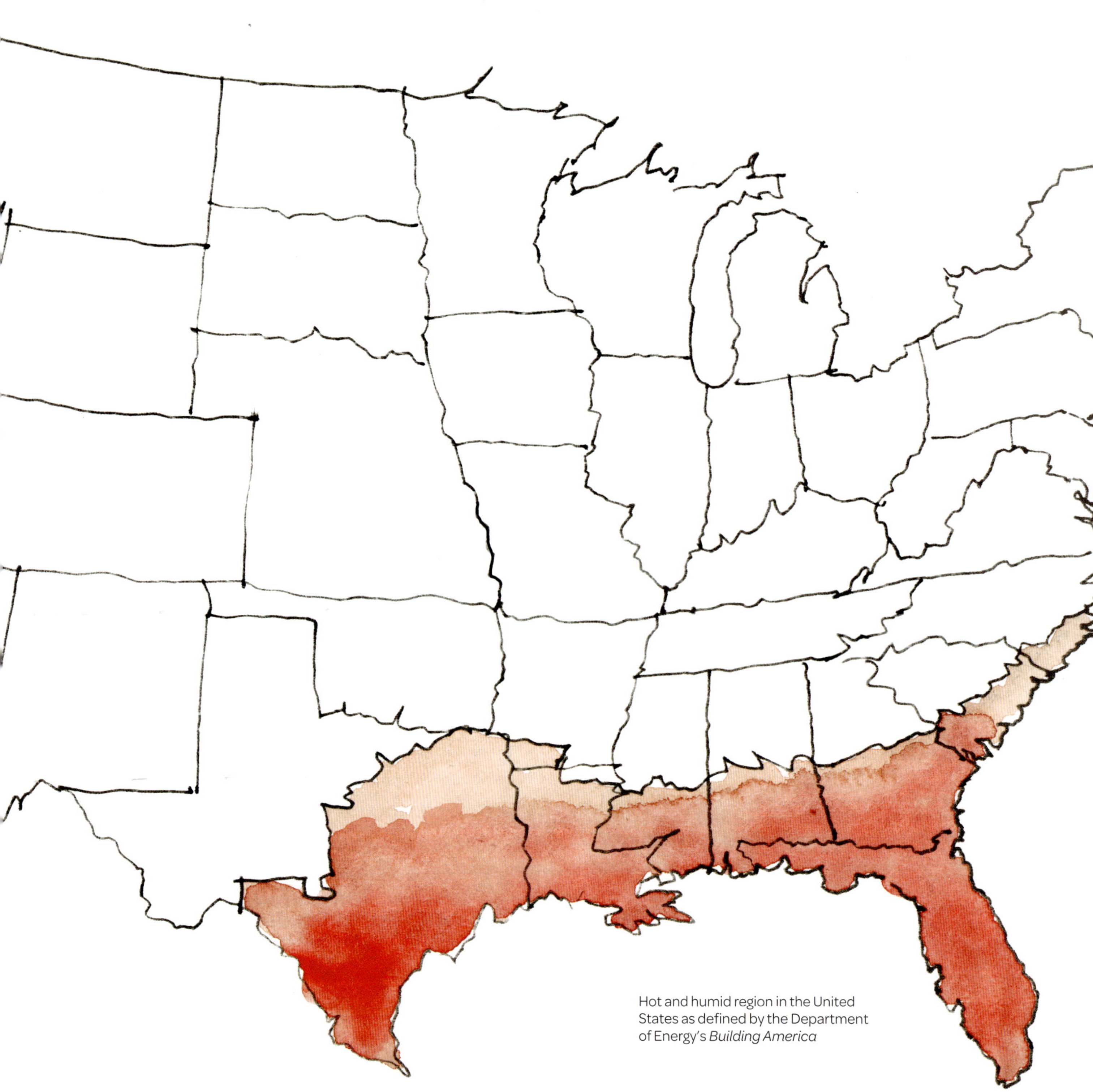

Hot and humid region in the United States as defined by the Department of Energy's *Building America*

FOREWORD

Who among us hasn't longed for a house that settles our needs, comforts and protects us, shelters us, and gives us peace? As we drive through the suburbs of the American South and the rest of the United States, however, too often we encounter overblown houses in a riot of styles that strive for individual identity. We wonder, How can any of this constellation of McMansions relate to our time and place? Is there a better way?

In the following pages, architects Jane and Michael Frederick offer an alternative to the developer mentality. *Contemporary Southern Vernacular: Creating Sustainable Houses for Hot, Humid Climates* grounds us in the realities of building in the green, enveloping warmth of the coastal lowlands. Admirably, they remind us of how our ancestors met this demanding landscape and structured housing that made living there not only possible but worthwhile. Early settlers discovered and replicated the passive techniques that still work: high ceilings to evacuate rising heat, walls that can accept and repel water and humidity, porches, orientation that shelters against harsh sunlight, dogtrots that encourage breezes. Those ideas still work today, and the Fredericks wisely trumpet the case for their revival.

At the same time, they fill in the diagram. In the twentieth century, the French architect Le Corbusier stated that a house is a "machine-à-habiter," a machine to live in. Jane and Michael accept that notion and show how contemporary planners and architects can design structures that work efficiently and well in this new century. Employing the scientific lessons of today's best building technology, architects and engineers can recapture the heat from the earth and sky, essentially recycling natural forces for our homes. Lower utility bills and greater human comfort can cohabit in our homes, allowing us to build in greater harmony with the world around us while feathering our own nests. Everyone wins, but it takes forethought, something these architects provide.

Jane and Michael ask relevant questions. How will a house first be seen? How does the vegetation affect the sunlight? Where do views occur? Seemingly direct and simple, these inquiries point to a methodology in planning that is sympathetic to the work of the late Christopher Alexander. In books such as *The Timeless Way of Building*, Alexander proposed that good planning can come about by asking a hierarchy of questions, from our place on planet Earth to how we approach the doors of our dwellings. By their own interrogatory method, Frederick and Frederick examine the architectural project holistically, from far approach and woodland setting to interior views from within. Clients, the inhabitants of this architectural dialogue, take part, and the result is often not a house on a hill, obvious and self-referential, but a home that is congruent, sympathetic, bespoke.

The proof lies in the houses themselves. The houses produced by the team at Frederick + Frederick, often constructed of simple board and batten, fit within the lowlands with minimal intrusion and a kind of natural modesty. The houses in the case studies might have been trumpeted in a four-color monograph, as many designers do. Instead, the Fredericks have thought about how they build in a fragile, desirable ecosystem and generously shared their ideas for a world in need of good design. Reading this book can educate a new generation of architects and their clients, opening the door and welcoming us in.

—Robert Ivy, FAIA, former editor in chief of *Architectural Record* and EVP/CEO of the American Institute of Architects

Columbus, Mississippi, September 2024

INTRODUCTION:
Our Sustainable, Resilient Home Design Journey

"With a fabulous house, things are just better."
—Michael Frederick

Well-designed homes create happier, healthier lives. Great home design not only honors the needs of the homeowners but connects them to the land and its history and also takes into account the home's natural setting. Southern vernacular architecture is our inspiration for designing homes around how people live, their joys and passions, and their land, while creating sustainable, resilient homes. Vernacular architecture was refined over generations to respond to the local climate, materials, and context. In hot, humid climates, the vernacular design developed to include south-facing porches, single-room-width plans running east to west, raised first floors, high ceilings, large overhangs, and other elements. We find that by starting with the vernacular concepts, we get a head start on sustainability.

We will explore the rich history of the vernacular further in the next chapter, but first it's important to understand the evolution of home building in the South during the twentieth century. Our journey into this history came through our own experiences. In our early years, we stumbled upon a major villain: moisture. In 2002, we had an eye-opener into the complexities of home design in hot, humid climates during two oceanfront home renovation projects on Hilton Head Island. The first home's project was replacing the exterior finish system. When we opened a wall, a swarm of termites flew out. To our horror, toxic mold had permeated the walls, and we had to act fast. One day, the homeowners were living in the house and the next, we had an abatement team in hazmat suits gutting the home.

The interior of the Hilton Head Island wall

We discovered that the home's synthetic exterior insulation finishing system (EIFS) had failed. It was initially designed as a waterproof exterior membrane, but its improper detailing and construction caused water and water vapor to seep behind the exterior wall through bad flashing, cracks, and fractures, so moisture didn't have a way to dry out. When improper detailing in hot, humid climates fails, it fails dramatically.

A few months later, we began work on another house. Again, we expected to complete only a relatively small renovation: kitchen, bath, and a small addition. When we pulled wood shingles off the wall for the addition, we found the same mold, mildew, and termites we'd encountered on the first project. Once again, we took the house down to the studs. This was an "Aha!" moment for us because both homes had been designed to code. Considering that fact, we asked ourselves: Why are these twenty-year-old houses failing and hazardous to their inhabitants despite being built to the current building code? What happened? How does the detailing of houses in a hot, humid climate need to be done differently?

We found our answers in the research of Joe Lstiburek, PhD, P.Eng., ASHRAE Fellow, now known as the dean of building science. That's when we discovered that all building codes everywhere had been written for colder, northern climates. Essentially, we were designing homes for a hot, humid climate but using building codes that didn't make sense. Joe even called the people who had developed the building methods and codes of the past one hundred years "cold-weather chauvinists." His discoveries flipped the building standards in the South, and we began to uncover how the industry went from building with the climate to ignoring it completely.

The transition from vernacular designs built for the hot, humid climates to houses failing after twenty years began with the home-building boom after World War II and the wide use of residential air-conditioning. To meet the massive demand for new homes for returning veterans, developers began to think differently about construction. In order to build homes faster, they developed modular components using premanufactured materials.

Instead of the old methods of exterior 1-by-6-inch wood sheathing and interior lath (narrow wooden slats) and plaster to build walls, they used premanufactured products such as Homasote, a fiberboard made from wood pulp and newspaper, or an asphalt-impregnated fiberboard for the exterior sheathing and drywall on the interior. However, the paper-based products were an inferior building material for hot, humid climates. Mold needs three things to thrive: moisture, oxygen, and something to eat. These materials gave mold everything it needed to eat (the old building method of wood, lath, and plaster wasn't appetizing to mold). Condensation from air-conditioning provided the moisture.

For speed and ease of construction, the building industry developed stock plans with 8-foot wall studs and sheet materials, effectively eliminating the tall ceilings of the Southern vernacular, which let heat rise. As suburbia grew and McMansions flourished, less and less attention was paid to the quality of construction. The 1970s oil embargo was the impetus for increased weatherization and insulation of houses to conserve energy. This created huge condensation problems in unconditioned, vented attics and vented crawl spaces in the hot, humid South. In the beachfront homes we renovated on Hilton Head, foil-faced fiberglass batt insulation compounded the mildew and mold problems, because it created a vapor barrier in the wrong location, essentially trapping moisture inside the walls of the homes.

The biggest change in building practices in the South came in 1992, in the aftermath of historic Category 5 Hurricane Andrew, when Florida established some of the toughest storm-specific building codes in the country. Most of the Coastal South followed its lead within a few years. The priority was to prevent buildings from blowing away. The resulting codes required that buildings had to be tied down from the roof to the foundation, while openings, such as windows, had to be protected from flying debris.

Once the buildings were secure, new problems were discovered when major storms hit these houses, bringing driving rain and pressure differentials in the home that allowed water infiltration. When you don't have a roof, you don't notice the other problems, so these were "new issues." In the early years of the 2000s, scientists such as Joe, together with the Department of Energy, began studying how to design buildings for different climates, and this led to their understanding of how to construct the building enclosure in hot, humid climates.

The building enclosure refers to the elements of a building that seal the outside environment from the inside—for example, its roof, doors, windows, floors, and walls. We will discuss more about the building enclosure in chapter 4.

After learning the significance of Joe's research and before the codes had changed to address different climates, we needed to petition the local building officials to allow us to detail the Hilton Head homes appropriately, using the most recent building science for our climate. We successfully obtained a variance from the code to build the homes the right way. This meant keeping the outside out and the inside in, making wall, roof, and floor systems tight enough to keep hot, humid air from coming inside and creating condensation.

Our Quonset Hut

As we discovered the brave new world of building in hot, humid climates, our journey to designing sustainable, resilient homes got personal. When we lived in downtown Beaufort, South Carolina, we dreamed about having a home on the marsh, a place where we could also have our office. One day, Michael bicycled by a guy who was hammering in a For Sale sign on a beautiful property. And that's how we found our current home, a Quonset hut we've lived in since 1992.

The authors' Quonset hut when they purchased the property in 1992

Quonset huts look like half cylinders lying on the ground. They were lightweight buildings used by the United States Navy during World War II because they could easily be shipped and assembled anywhere. When we first bought the hut, we planned on tearing it down because it was so nasty—its exterior had been painted a dull army green, the interior had shag carpeting, the bathrooms were old and in need of repair, and the previous owners had dropped the ceilings so the interior felt dark and confined.

Then one night, Michael said, "You know what? We could have curved ceilings." So that just sold us. We loved the idea. And we also loved how people would stop by and share their memories about the Quonset hut, which had been built right after World War II. Our home was part of the neighborhood, and that warmed us to our renovation project idea. Reusing and reworking

an existing structure is always less expensive and more sustainable than starting from scratch, so the Quonset hut became our ultimate recycling project. We were about to turn a tin can into a home.

Our house is our laboratory, and we always have some project in the works. At the beginning of the hut remodel, we tore everything out and took the hut down to its metal shell. Then we did some structural work to tie it down and ensure the hut's resilience in the event of a hurricane. We'll talk more about our home remodel in the case study for chapter 5: "Materials for Health, Durability & Aesthetics."

Our goals were probably a lot like yours when we started designing homes in the South. We wanted a home that would grow with our family and allow us to stay in our home for our lifetime. Sustainability has

The Quonset hut after the renovation.
Courtesy of Dickson Dunlap

always been important to us as a way to honor our own connection to the land. Resiliency—or how homes can be designed to weather hurricanes, lightning, flooding, and other threats—has been increasingly more important as our weather patterns have changed over the years. We also wanted to invest in a resilient, sustainable, beautiful home.

When you move into an existing house, you make the house work for you. But if you're building a custom home or doing a major renovation, you get to think about how you live and design the house around your lifestyle. For example, if you want to be awakened by the sun, then we design your home with the principal bedroom on the east side so you get that morning light. If you are interested in your home growing with your family, we pay attention to spaces that can adapt and change to those growing needs, such as turning nurseries into sitting rooms or bedrooms into suites for aging relatives. Honoring what is most important to you as your family grows and changes in your home and incorporating those dreams into your home's design not only makes life better but will also save you money.

Your home should enhance your life; therefore, you want it to be sustainable, healthy, and resilient. Building in a hot, humid climate is a mystery to a lot of people who come from colder climates and even to people in the Southern building industry. Make sure you're working with professionals who understand building in a hot, humid climate—and someone who can stand up to contractors who have been unknowingly using at-risk construction methods in the South. These people can frequently say their methods have "worked just fine." But they haven't. Building science has advanced dramatically in the past twenty years, and many in the industry just aren't up to speed in sustainable, resilient home design.

This porch was designed to enjoy the sunrise view over the pond.
Courtesy of Kim Smith

Maybe you're an architect in the South who is confronting similar issues like we did. Or maybe you're a homeowner looking to make a substantial renovation. Perhaps you're someone just starting out with a dream of building your own home in the South. Whoever you are and whatever your dream, we hope this will be your helpful guide to understanding how to build the home of your dreams in a hot, humid climate.

How to Use This Book

In the following chapters, we explore the vernacular in two parts. In section I, we define the vernacular traditions in a historical context. In section II, we discuss sustainable strategies for hot, humid climates, using our specific home designs as examples. We'll look at elements such as site studies, building in geographically challenging situations, and the building enclosure. We'll discuss using durable, healthy, and aesthetically pleasing materials, as well as how to get to net-zero emissions and its return on investment, plus various resiliency issues such as survivability, longevity of materials, and aging in place (the ability to live in your home for your lifetime).

Having a comfortable home custom designed to grow with your changing needs and lifestyles isn't some pie-in-the-sky idea. We did it, and you can too. While mold issues began our building science research journey, we've advanced beyond designing homes for hot, humid climates to include resilient, sustainable design that helps our clients age in place. Designing with the Southern vernacular isn't only good for our planet; it's affordable and much easier than you might think. We are honored to be part of your design journey and hope the ideas and discoveries in this book will inspire you to build your dream house in whatever part of the South you call home.

SECTION I:

Vernacular Tradition MEETS Contemporary DESIGN

CHAPTER 1
A Southern Vernacular Primer

"Traditional (vernacular) buildings are summaries of problems already solved."

—Thomas Hubka in "Just Folks Designing: Vernacular Designers and the Generation of Form" from the book *Common Places: Readings in American Vernacular Architecture,* edited by Dell Upton and John Michael Vlach, University of Georgia Press

We like this quote because it speaks to the way the vernacular forms are generative. The wisdom the vernacular imparts not only has been our inspiration but has also become the foundation for our contemporary design solutions. In the following pages, we are going to explore the unique characteristics of vernacular houses for hot, humid climates and how those characteristics were incorporated into seven different building forms—single house, Creole cottage, I-house, shotgun, Beaufort freedman's cottage, T-house, and dogtrot—and will discuss how they inform our design throughout the rest of the book.

It is important to note that many historic houses are not vernacular houses, because they were often built from imported plan books of English or Italian designs. The *Encyclopedia of Vernacular Architecture of the World* defines vernacular architecture in this way:

> Comprising the dwellings and all other buildings of the people. Related to their environmental contexts and available resources, they are customarily owner—or community—built, utilizing traditional technologies. All forms of vernacular architecture are built to meet specific needs, accommodating the values, economies and ways of life of the cultures that produce them.

Courtesy of Dickson Dunlap

A Hot, Humid Vernacular Primer

The Southern vernacular in hot, humid climates used many common techniques to cool the home and protect it from harsh conditions:

- Houses are one room wide and have the narrow side on the east and west. This orientation reduces the heat gain from the sun rising in the east and setting in the west.
- Cross breezes provide great air circulation throughout the home when the windows are open.
- Porches are always on the south and often on the other sides as well. They are used to promote air circulation between rooms in the house and also protect the home from driving rain. Porches were used for circulation passages too, since there were often not interior hallways.
- Homes are oriented to capture the prevailing breezes.
- All the houses have raised first floors, usually on brick piers. This is significant for two reasons—the breeze is better higher off the ground, and the raised foundation protects the home from floodwaters and damp soil.
- Tall ceilings allow heat to rise, away from living spaces.

Sustainably Connects People to Nature

Porches were much more than a key way the vernacular eased the crushing heat; they also brought families together. We clearly remember when we were children and our extended families sat on the porch while everyone told stories. Like many Southerners, they were great storytellers. Jane remembers how her grandaunts would get so mad at how her grandfather embellished his stories that they would call him out on all the lies he told. Enjoying each other while we relax on our porch each night is more than a way to connect with the land and marvel at its beauty. Our porch connects us with our past. We think Rick Bragg says it best in his book *My Southern Journey*:

> They say a kitchen is the heart of a house, but I believe the porch is its soul. From the very steps, you knew if you were welcome or not, knew everything you needed to know about the people inside. My grandmother Velma welcomed the whole world there on those boards, except for a few insurance men and anyone with a pamphlet. . . .
>
> The porch was always cool, as if summer stopped at that first step. The house was like a furnace in the hot months, and the porch, perched in the foothills of the Alabama highland, was a cool oasis in the heat. There was no electric light on the porch, no bright bulb to draw insects or add to the heat. Porches were for talking, and rocking babies, and cutting okra and snapping beans and telling lies. A body did not need a lot of light for that, and—if the lying got out of hand—the darker the better.
>
> I remember its scent, an ambrosia of black coffee mixing in the wind with the sweet smell of canned milk, and honeysuckle, and snuff. It made the babies sneeze. In the evening, the children would retreat beneath the porch to be away from their mamas and daddies but still not quite away, to be with them and yet not right with them, which is a delicious thing that only a child really understands.

The porch is only one example of how the vernacular speaks to us. Sitting on our porch is one way for us to remember how important it is that we honor our connection to each other and our environment. Historically, Southern vernacular home designs have developed to work well with, not against, the hot, humid climate. Its materials not only reflected where people lived but also became an outward expression of their connection to the land.

Homes were typically constructed of brick, cypress, and pine. Since cypress is rot resistant, people used it for roof and wall sheathing, exterior siding, and porch ceilings. Heart pine was used to build structural components of the homes. Its durability made heart pine ideal for wood floors. Sourcing local materials is more sustainable than using nonnative materials. Importing nonnative materials not only costs time and money, but these materials also don't reflect the spirit of the land and region, creating homes that feel out of place.

History and Forms of the Southern Vernacular

The long history of the vernacular for hot, humid climates includes the coastal areas of North Carolina, South Carolina, Florida, Georgia, Mississippi, Alabama, Louisiana, and East Texas. The earliest recorded history of structures in this region began in the sixteenth century with the Seminoles, who built *chickees* (a Seminole word for house), which were raised up out of the marshes on cypress logs with open walls that provided good air circulation.

From the beginning, the Southern colonies were a mixture of different nationalities. Colonists from England, France, the Netherlands, Germany, Ireland, Scotland, Switzerland, and the Iberian Peninsula and enslaved Africans all contributed to and adapted to the New World, while also learning from the Indigenous Americans. It was more of a mosaic than a tapestry, because each nationality tended to settle in communities with their fellow countrymen.

The Spanish settled in Florida and into the Carolinas; the French along the Gulf, in Mobile and New Orleans. Charleston, South Carolina (originally Charles Town), was more cosmopolitan, with English, Scots, and Sephardic Jews from the Iberian Peninsula. In South Carolina, the Swiss settled in Purrysburg on the Savannah River, the Germans on the Edisto River in Orangeburg, and French Huguenots settled in New Bordeaux on Long Cane Creek.

As Europeans moved to the Southern colonies, they built their homes by using the construction methods from their homeland. However, this could be problematic. For example, the Germans used a traditional timber frame, pier, and clapboard construction. As the archeologist J. W. Joseph discovered, the Germans struggled to come to terms with the problems of such innate styles in their new termite-infested, humid, Southern environment. Their homes fell apart after only a handful of years.

The French first came to Mobile, Alabama, and then migrated to Biloxi, Mississippi, and eventually traveled on to New Orleans, Louisiana. The shotgun house and the Creole cottage became part of their vernacular. The French stayed in the coastal areas since the interior of the country had been involved in many land battles between different countries and Indigenous Americans. Plantation houses, larger homes with a wraparound porches, were built along the Gulf of Mexico and up the Mississippi River. Since Louisiana was the hottest, most humid part of the South, the French used wraparound porches to beat the heat.

The shotgun house and single house had African origins. The shotgun house found in New Orleans came through Haiti and was the house form of freed, formerly enslaved people. They introduced the raised ceiling and first-floor cross circulation, which we use in our contemporary designs today. Cross circulation was one way to keep bugs at bay, since bugs don't linger in breezes.

Charleston Single House

The single house comes from Ghana via the West Indies. The traditional homes of the coastal West Africans, especially the homes of chiefs, were usually a single room wide with a side porch that also served as a living area. In the city of Charleston, South Carolina, these single houses were densely set on narrow lots. The homes featured porches built on the south side. The thin side of the home, the single-room width of the home, faced the street. At the end of the porch was a wall with an exterior front door. Typically, a carriage entrance with a carriage house would be located next to the single house.

The first Charleston single houses were built after the great fire of 1740. Before then, homes were built low to the ground, without a side porch, so they lacked the air circulation needed to cool the home. After the great fire, Charleston homeowners rebuilt and designed the sustainable single house. Today, the streets of Charleston are lined with the beautiful alternating sight of house-porch-house-porch, with magnificently decorated doors that open to the street. Charleston's single houses are a good example of how the vernacular form is used for large, very formal and ornate houses and also very small and simple houses.

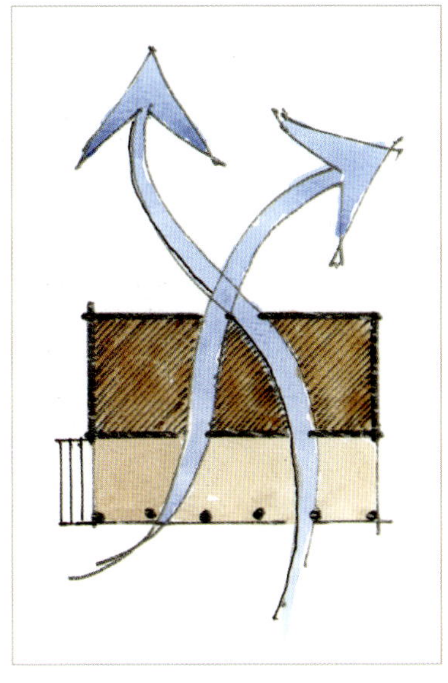

Charleston single house air circulation

Thomas Rhodes House, circa 1790, Beaufort, South Carolina

I-house

A typical Southern house was the plantation plain-style—or "I"—house, so named because of its tall, narrow profile. This house was two stories with a gable roof on the short side and a shed-roofed (one sloping side) one-story porch in front. The I-house resembles the single house in its floor plan; however, the entrance is located on the long side of the porch. For example, if the porch has three bays, then the front doors would be placed in the middle bay. This is also called the plantation plain-style, since it was a common house on the plantations throughout the South.

This simple house was one room deep, andmany had an open center hall. According to Lane Mills in his Architecture of the Old South series, the main innovation of the I-house was its folding doors in the center hall, which was an early version of the now-popular folding-door walls. There were also masonry chimneys on each end of the house. High ceilings allowed the heat to rise, providing a more comfortable environment. The single-room width allowed the second-floor sleeping rooms to have ventilation on three sides. Occasionally, there would be a double porch on the front of the house. Kitchens were usually in a separate building behind the home; this kept the heat from the fireplace out of the main house and also protected the main house in the event of a kitchen fire.

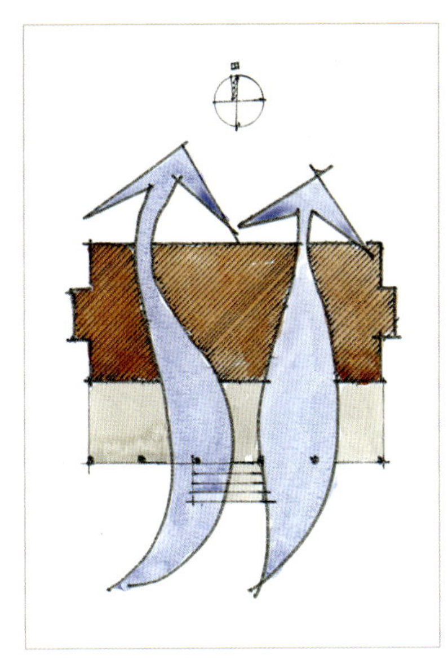

I-house
air circulation

Creole Cottage

Creole architecture is a combination of French and Spanish influences that evolved in the New World. Creole refers to people descended from Europeans and Africans. Over a period of time, these settlers built homes from New Orleans to Mobile that were suited for the hot, humid climate. The unique house form they constructed is called the Creole cottage.

While there are different variations of the Creole cottage, the basic form has a raised foundation to keep living areas above the usually damp ground, a wraparound porch, and a double-pitched roof. Steep roofs help shed the driving rains. Typically, the cottages were one room wide and three rooms long (the center room being the largest) with interconnecting doors. These houses are distinguished by the lack of interior halls and stairways. All the occupants' circulation occurred on the porches.

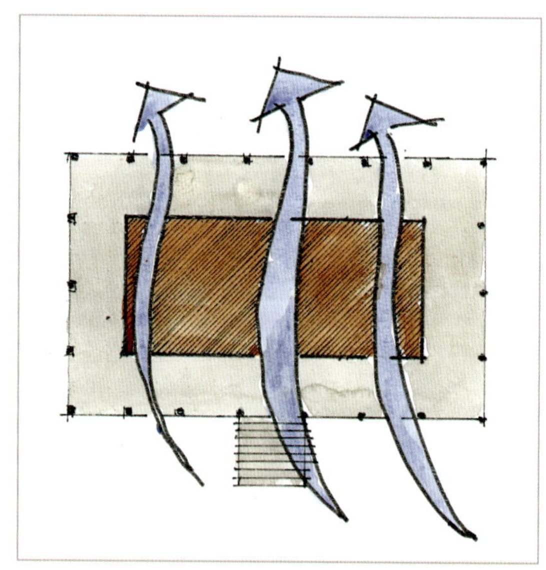

Creole cottage
air circulation

Shotgun

A narrow one-story rectangular house, the shotgun is one room wide (about 12 to 14 feet) and three to five rooms deep, with no hallway. It has high ceilings to let heat rise and a front door on the thin side, which faces the street. The front facade usually has three tall openings, one door and two windows, with shutters for ventilation and privacy. The roof extends over a small front porch that opens into the living room. Bedrooms are in the middle of the house, with the kitchen in the back. They are built off the ground for air circulation, and the long, narrow house provides excellent cross ventilation.

John Michael Vlach, one of the nation's premier scholars on African American folk art and plantation architecture, determined that the shotgun house has an African architectural heritage. It came to New Orleans via Haiti from the West African country of Dahomey, now the Republic of Benin. Vlach discovered a similar vernacular form in Dahomey. The shotgun house appeared in New Orleans around the same time as the influx of free Blacks from Haiti.

Haiti, once known as Saint-Domingue, was the first nation to permanently ban slavery and the slave trade. In 1791, a thirteen-year revolution began against French rule. The Black revolutionaries crushed Napoleon's army and afterward proclaimed the nation of Haiti (the original Indigenous name of the island). During the revolution, a terrible fire destroyed most of the island's major city, Cap Français (present-day Cap Haïtien), causing ten thousand Haitian refugees to flee. During this time, Haitians immigrated to many North American cities en masse, including New Orleans. While the Haitian immigrants were seen as a threat to the stability of an economy that depended on the slave trade, they found community with the French-speaking Creoles.

There are several theories about how the shotgun form got its name. Vlach suggests that it came from the Fon people of Dahomey, who had a word *to-gun*, which means "place of assembly," and that *to-gun* was misinterpreted to mean shotgun. The more popular theory is that the name came from the fact that if you opened all the doors in the house, you could shoot a gun and the bullet would pass cleanly through every room of the house, from front to back.

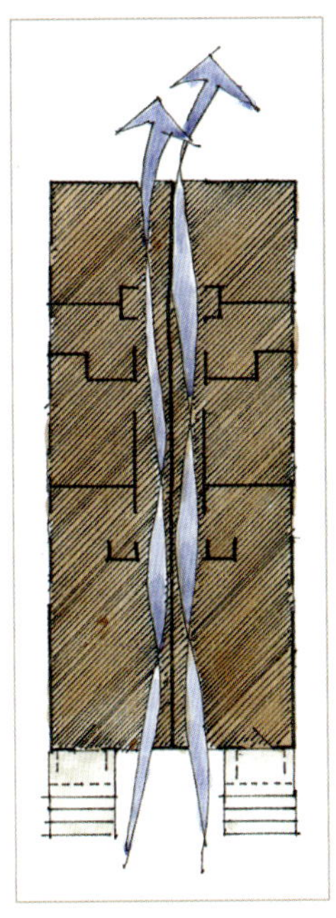

Shotgun
air circulation

The building on the right is based on the form of the freedman's cottage. *Courtesy of John McManus*

Beaufort Freedman's Cottage

> "Everyday life and colonial South Carolina reflected the collision and blending of cultures—European, West African, and Indian. These cultures not only interacted with one another and were changed, but all of them had to deal with the reality of the environment." —Walter Edgar, *South Carolina: A History*

Freedman cottages were built after the Civil War and are modest one-story, two-room houses, also known as a "hall-and-parlor house." The cottage has a front porch and is one room deep and two rooms wide. The hall (the bigger room) was the public room, and the parlor (the smaller room) was the sleeping room. They had high ceilings and often had a sleeping loft. Over time, people added small additions with shed roofs to the rear of the home. The kitchen was typically in a separate building. It was very common to do a lot of living in the yard.

The Beaufort freedman's cottage was built by the Gullah Geechee people of the Sea Islands of South Carolina and Georgia (the Gullah Geechee are descendants of the enslaved Africans). Their vernacular included painting their porch ceilings a special shade of blue that was based on the color of the indigo dye that was grown in the Lowcountry. The color, sometimes called "haint blue," is found in Southern coastal cities such as Savannah, Georgia, and Charleston, South Carolina, and is still used to paint porch ceilings today.

"Haint" is a colloquial way of saying ghost, because some people believed that the paint color also kept ghosts and hags at bay. The blue paint was believed to trick the haints by preventing them from entering the home. If they thought the paint was the sky, the haints would fly up away from the home, and if they thought the paint was water, the ghosts would simply not enter the home (it was a popular belief that ghosts didn't cross water).

We wanted to know more about the history of freedman cottages, so we sat down with Larry Rowland, the author of three books on the history of Beaufort County, South Carolina, spanning from 1514 to 2006. He shared with us that freed slaves bought their land inexpensively at government tax auctions after the Civil War and were required to build a house of some sort on the land.

Over the years, many of the cottages disappeared. A great deal of them didn't survive simply due to poor maintenance. Also, the deadly Sea Islands Hurricane of 1893 simply washed away the freedman cottages. Over two thousand people died in that hurricane (by drowning) when a massive storm surge covered the Sea Islands, and another twenty thousand were left homeless, since most buildings on the barrier islands were damaged beyond repair. When walking the streets of Beaufort, we can point to places where the catastrophic storm literally shaped our town. This history has made us passionate about resiliency in home design.

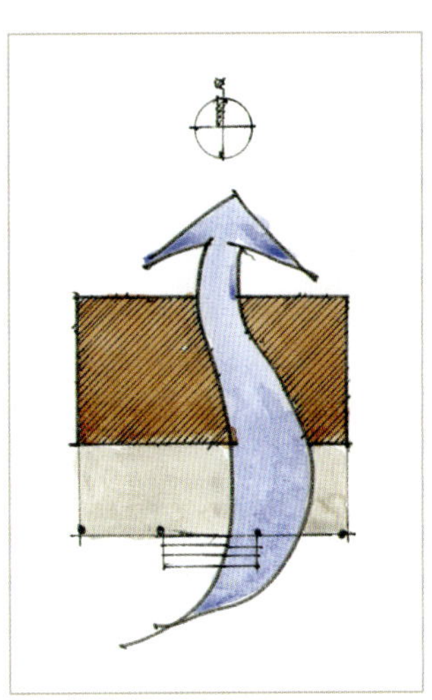

Freedman cottage air circulation

T-house

The T-house was typically larger than the other vernacular forms. It had a porch on each of its two stories. The porches wrapped on the east, south, and west sides of the home. Usually, the door on the north side had a small covered porch.

The T-house is unique to Beaufort, South Carolina, and was so named because the inside of the home forms the shape of a "T." The staircase to the second floor is located at the junction of the T, which provides vertical circulation for air and people. The public area forms the front of the T, and the sleeping chambers are located in the back of the house in the crossbar of the T (*see diagram*). However, at the time that this form originated, rooms weren't necessarily defined by the ways people used them, so people changed how they used their rooms depending on the season. For example, people would move their bedroom from one place in the house to another to benefit from seasonal microclimates. The T-house also had sleeping porches to take advantage of the better outdoor breezes.

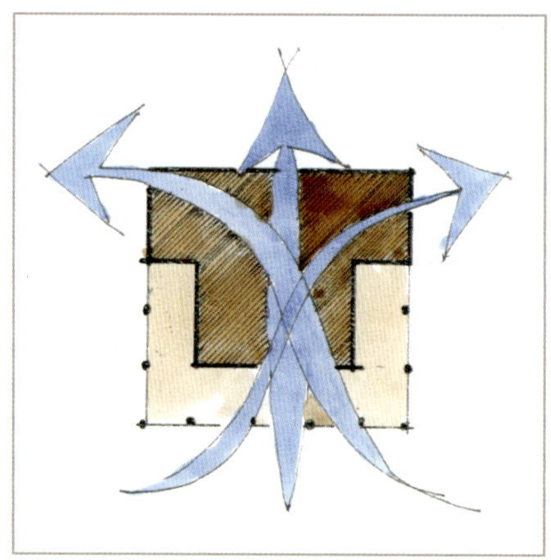

T-house air circulation

OPPOSITE: Front (north) elevation of a Beaufort T-house (*above*) and rear (south) elevation of a Beaufort T-house (*below*)

Dogtrot

In his book *Cotton Kingdom*, Frederick Law Olmsted described a dogtrot he visited in Louisiana in 1850: "The house was a double log cabin—two log erections, that is, joined by one long roof, leaving an open space between. A gallery, extending across the whole front, serves for a pleasant sitting room in summer." Olmsted, the founder of American landscape architecture and co-designer of New York City's Central Park, had taken a few pre–Civil War tours through the South and wrote about it for the *New York Times*.

The dogtrot is traditionally a modest, one-story home commonly found throughout the South, even in northern Alabama and Tennessee. Early European settlers would start by building one room, then adding a second room and connecting the two under one roof. Usually, one building was the sleeping area and the other was the living area. Quite often, the kitchen was housed in a separate building out back due to the hot climate (and to guard against fire).

This form uses the middle open space between the two buildings to channel breezes by using the Bernoulli effect, a principle of physics where a change in pressure causes a better circular flow of air. In this form, outside breezes speed up as they flow through the channel created by the porch. And so, the home provides a very pleasant, shady place to sit during hot, humid afternoons. The form is thought to have gotten its name because dogs like to sit in the center space.

The following case study is a great example of our contemporary dogtrot design. Unique to the design, the center hall dogtrot space has folding doors on the front and back where the home can be completely opened to nature.

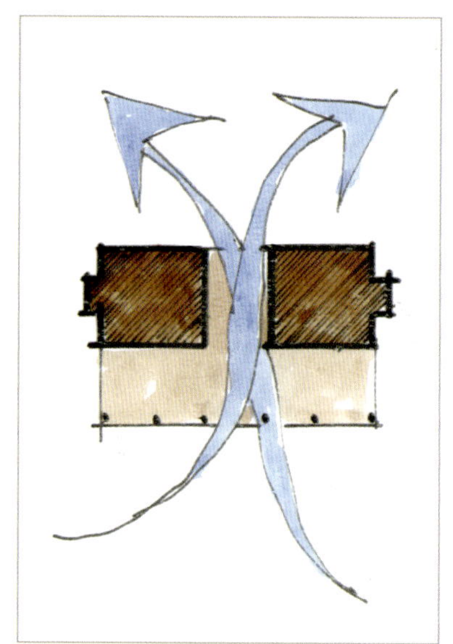

Dogtrot air circulation

OPPOSITE: Contemporary dogtrot

The center hall of the dogtrot opens with a large folding door with retractable screens. *All photographs in this case study courtesy of Helen Norman*

CASE STUDY: CONTEMPORARY DOGTROT

This house is a true Southern-style dogtrot with a modern take, designed to optimize natural cooling while delivering expansive views, connecting the owners to their wooded surroundings. The lot is on a high bluff overlooking the May River in the development of Palmetto Bluff. We set the house back 80 feet from the bluff to provide a natural buffer and oriented it to capture the prevailing southwestern breezes. The natural landscape is composed of mostly native plant material and a few flowering nonnatives, particularly in the small formal garden between the house and garage. An existing live oak creates an archway that centers on the front door. The house is placed as far to the north as the site allows, to give ample space on the south for a bocce court and fire pit among the native vegetation. The principal bedroom is on the northern side, with lots of windows to take advantage of the view to the river. The public rooms, the kitchen and family room, are on the south to connect to the exterior living and to allow for more privacy from their neighbors.

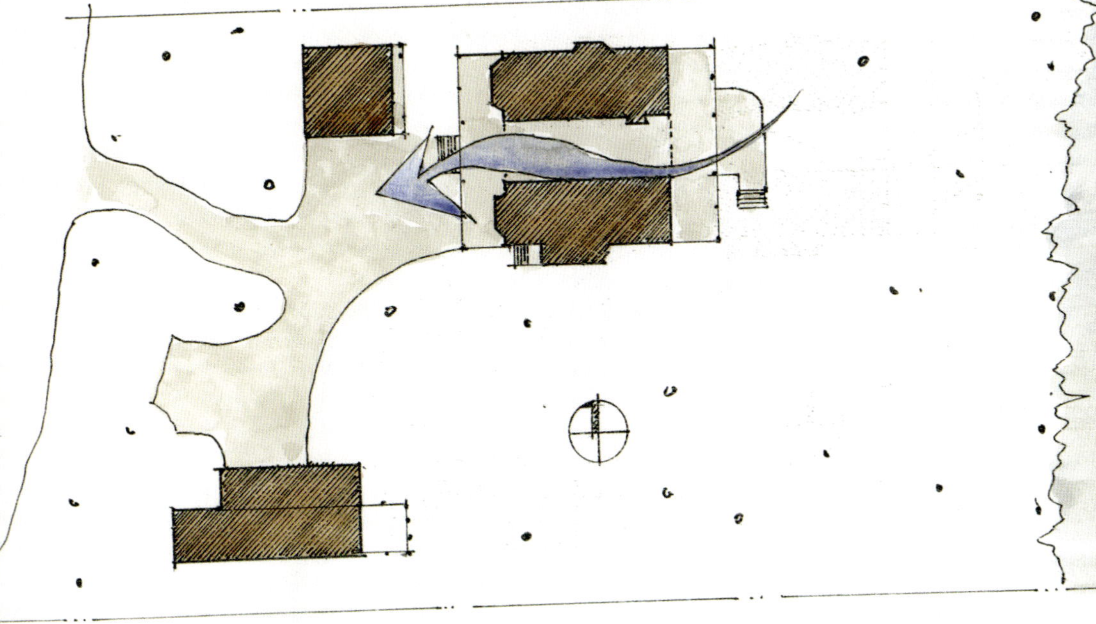

Our clients loved the idea of building a contemporary dogtrot—especially the concept of an open exterior space in the middle of their home—because the design looked and felt like it belonged on the property.

But it was the open middle space of the dogtrot home that was the unique part of the home's design. Compared to a traditional dogtrot, this center breezeway can be opened to the natural breezes or closed with large folding doors and air-conditioned. Our clients can gauge the proper conditions for opening the large folding door for natural air circulation by the dew point, which measures the amount of water vapor in the air. When the dew point is 60 degrees or below, the conditions are right for natural air circulation. In the South, it is possible to open homes to fresh air four or five months out of the year.

Front of the dogtrot

The dining room is in the dogtrot space.

In the home, the interior walls on either side of the classic dogtrot opening are exterior walls, so the heat pump can run in the side interior spaces while doors in the middle of the house fold completely open on both the front and back. When open, this creates the classic dogtrot form: One opening runs from the front door with a retractable screen to the screened-in porch at the back of the house. In this way, the home literally lets the outside in, allowing the clients to enjoy natural breezes inside the home while spending time in nature. The home design beautifully connects them to the land and provides wonderful ways to enjoy the natural setting.

The house is sided with reverse board-and-batten cypress siding. This detail creates an airspace that allows the wall to dry between the water barrier layer and the siding. Notice that every window and door are laid out so the narrow batten is the jamb trim. The owners are boat lovers, so the natural stained-wood windows, doors, and ceilings appealed to their aesthetic.

An abundance of natural light is provided with north- and east-facing skylights, high windows in the open dogtrot space, large windows, and the glass folding doors. A zinc roof provided a soft heat-reflective surface that varies its color as the light changes throughout the day.

The wall between the kitchen and dogtrot space is an exterior wall with windows.

In the next chapter, we'll explore site design and examine how to overcome challenges that may arise when designing your house for your property or when you might need to consider how to leverage a site to make your home renovation project more sustainable and resilient.

The fireplace is in the dogtrot space and opens to the screen porch on the rear.

Contemporary Dogtrot: Sustainable Strategies

VERNACULAR

- Dogtrot
- Sited to capture prevailing winds
- High ceilings
- Large overhangs

CONTEMPORARY

- Reverse board and batten that creates an airspace
- Conditioned crawl and attic spaces
- Local cypress siding
- Impact glass
- Reclaimed heart pine floor
- Local cypress ceilings
- 17.9 SEER heat pump with ERV
- Blower door test
- Designed for 140 mph winds
- Limited lawn
- Native landscape and rain garden

Completed: 2008

Builder: Bay 10 Ventures
Hilton Head, South Carolina

Landscape Architect:
Verdant Enterprises
Savannah, Georgia

MENUS
DOG BISCUITS
ENGLISH BREAKFAST
CHEESE
SUNDAY

CHAPTER 2
Listening to the Land

"Let us take a minute and dream about what this could be."

—Robert Marvin,
Fellow of America Society of Landscape Architects (FASLA)

"When the design of a house has grown out of the uniqueness of its site, it will seem as natural and as integral a part of the whole as trees are a part of the forest."

—Max Jacobson et al., *Patterns of Home*

Early in Michael's career, he was mentored by Robert Marvin, FASLA, a landscape architect who was the son of the caretaker on Bonnie Doone Plantation, which encompassed 15,000 acres of natural beauty in the Lowcountry of South Carolina. Robert often told us that our ancestors lived their lives enveloped in nature, and they needed their homes to be cocoons. He believed that modern society had been alienated from nature by technology and that our houses and landscapes needed to be built so that we can reconnect to the rhythms of nature.

Michael and Robert met on an architectural review board in the 1990s. Sometimes, when people would submit plans to the board that didn't engage the site, Marvin would stand up and say, "Let us take a minute and dream about what this could be." Then he would wax poetic about the native trees, wind direction, sun angles, and wildlife and about how the new homeowners could become part of nature rather than separated from its beauty. Marvin always made the projects better because he would inspire homeowners and architects to resubmit home designs that honored their property.

There are many design and environmental benefits to our projects when we don't force our designs onto the sites they occupy, and instead listen to the land and let it inform the design. Taking your land into account in this way isn't the woo-woo, far-out thing that some might think. By leveraging the beauty of the land, and all that it has to offer, into the design of the home, its value increases.

A home's physical site is one of the most important parts of its design, but this is often overlooked. That's because homeowners can focus only on the home itself, forgetting about the land it sits on. That's understandable; after all, it's exciting to build or renovate your dream home. Likewise, home

Courtesy of Jeff Amberg

builders can also have competing interests. They often choose to ignore the land in favor of building as many houses per acre as possible, which can lead to the destruction of native plants and trees. And so, the land—what we think is the star of the show—becomes an afterthought or risks getting ignored completely.

When a house is designed in harmony with the land, it looks like it belongs there—because it does. In this chapter, we will explore how a home and its owners can truly belong to their land in ways that not only complement their lifestyle and surroundings but also foster their health and wellness.

Nature's Health Benefits

Early settlers had to live with the elements. There was no other way. Today, with all the technology that has been developed in home design, we've become separated from nature. While technology has given us some wonderful ways to live comfortably despite the harsh environment, our innate connection to the land is so visceral that we often miss the opportunity to experience the wind in our hair and the sun on our backs in our everyday life. Designing contemporary homes using the Southern vernacular can help us listen to the land.

Biophilia

Edward O. Wilson introduced a hypothesis in his book *Biophilia*, where he explored the positive health effects of our connection to nature, stating, "Our natural affinity for life—biophilia—is the very essence of our humanity and binds us to all other living species." Some examples of biophilic design include providing natural light, using natural finishes such as wood and stone, and incorporating water features such as ponds and fountains. These biophilic design features can help alleviate anxiety, reduce blood pressure, improve cognitive performance, and improve sleep. Other health benefits include boosting immune systems, supporting mental and emotional health, creating social connections, and aiding in physical recovery.

Alex Wilson, founding editor of *Environmental Building News*, a newsletter about environmentally sustainable building practices, has said that "biophilia, or human beings' inherent love for nature, has been called the missing link in sustainable design." From an environmental standpoint, biophilic features foster an appreciation of nature, which, in turn, should lead to greater protection of natural areas, eliminate pollution, and maintain a clean environment (from "Biophilia in Practice: Buildings That Connect People with Nature" by Alex Wilson, buildinggreen.com).

Alex Wilson continues exploring the long, storied health benefits of connecting to nature:

> As long as 2,000 years ago, according to Richard Louv in the book *Last Child in the Woods* (Algonquin Books, 2005), Chinese Taoists recognized that gardens and greenhouses were beneficial to health. Leonard [Meager], writing in the *English Gardener* in [1688], recommended spending time in a garden: "There is no better way to preserve your health." In 1859, the pioneering British nurse Florence Nightingale wrote in *Notes on Nursing* (reprinted by Scholarly Publishing Office, University of Michigan Library, 2005) that "variety of form and brilliancy of color in the objects presented to patients are an actual means of recovery."

Natural wood has biophilia qualities.

What Wilson uncovers in these examples is the well-documented need of humans to connect with nature wherever they are. And where better to connect with nature than at home? Wilson describes the various ways that biophilic design can be incorporated into design:

> By considering biophilic design strategies very early in the design process, opportunities relating to building siting, architectural form, internal layout, interior design, and landscaping can more easily be achieved. . . . This strategy encourages building occupants to explore, discover, and learn from the complexities of nature. . . . Visually, ecologically, historically, and culturally connecting a building to the locale helps connect occupants to a place and, in doing so, inspires them to protect that place.

By focusing on tying our designs to the land, our clients improve their health through better connections with nature.

This courtyard is designed around the massive live oak tree, creating an internal view. *Courtesy of Kim Smith*

The Power of Views: Shakkei

One of the most compelling ways we connect to a site is by admiring its views. Long views of rivers, oceans, or mountains are very peaceful and relaxing. They quiet our mind and fill our spirit, easing any tensions of the day.

But what if the site doesn't have these views? Even when sites don't provide natural views, we can create them. For example, even though our home has wonderful natural views, we created a courtyard that invites our guests into nature. Other ways to create views include features such as fountains, specimen trees, or garden statues. Creating moments such as these on your property—places for you to sit and enjoy its surroundings—is priceless. Even the smallest of spaces can be designed to tie you to nature through beautiful views.

There are other important ways to add views to your property. The Japanese concept of *shakkei* (sha-kay-ee) introduces the idea of the borrowed view and is often incorporated in Japanese gardens. The intention behind shakkei is to avoid an extravagantly designed space and trick the eye into thinking that the natural elements located outside the property are part of the garden. What do we mean by a borrowed view when designing homes? A borrowed view might come from the wildflowers of the East Texas Hill Country, the live oak tree on your neighbor's property, the rolling green hills of a golf course, or the ever-changing grasses of a nearby Lowcountry marsh.

In addition to avoiding gaudiness, shakkei offers other benefits. It's relatively economical, since it encourages residents to work with elements that are already on-site, and it allows for the illusion of an effortless harmony between the garden and the surrounding nature, which has become the defining characteristic of Japanese gardens (from "Japanese Words We Can't Translate: Shakkei—the Essence of Japanese Garden Design," tokyoweekender.com). Expand your awareness beyond your own property and see what views you can capture. Almost every home we design with a long view uses the concept of the borrowed view, such as the case study at the end of this chapter, Riverfront Home.

The designer incorporated a borrowed view in the Isui-en Garden in Nara, Japan.

The marsh is a borrowed view
from this outdoor living space.

Site Studies

We come from families who connected with the land, and with each other, through the tall tales told on porches come nightfall. So, connecting our clients to the land through home designs that incorporate meaningful outdoor spaces is our passion.

We begin our home designs with a site study, also known as a site analysis. A site study is documented on a scale drawing dedicated to examining the site's important climate, geographic, historical, legal, and infrastructure issues. It also helps to map out the microclimates within a site and determines how to take advantage of those elements. The site study is the key to understanding how our clients and their homes can optimally relate to the land and create a healing connection to nature.

We enhance our understanding of the land by studying the site analytically and emotionally. We accomplish this by first obtaining a tree and topographical survey through the services of a professional surveyor. We then spend time on the site during different times of day, weather conditions, and seasons. These visits help us notice various aspects of the property.

When you conduct these visits, you will become more familiar with your land. When you visit the site, ask yourself these questions:

- How does it feel at different times of day?
- What's the lighting like?
- What attributes of the land make it unique?
- What natural elements can you leverage to enhance the design of the home and your connection with nature?

Some other things to observe on your site include noise issues, aromas and odors, air quality (dust), any natural vegetation that can remain, and the location of any neighbors and their activity on surrounding lots—especially those with condenser units and terraces. Lighting effects, such as reflections and absorption, are also important to note. For example, observe how the sun penetrates the tree coverage. Is the land a deep forest of dappled light? Or is it open to plentiful sunlight? The site study is the key to fully exploring all that needs to be observed and documented.

GOING DEEPER WITH YOUR SITE STUDY

We begin our study of the site by obtaining a tree and topographic survey, prepared by a licensed surveyor. The survey should include the following:

- Legal boundaries
- Topographic contours
- Utility or other easements
- Footprints of existing structures and fences
- Location and types of trees with the trunk diameter over 6 inches at 4 feet from the ground
- Utility connection locations
- Existing septic tank and field
- Roads and sidewalks
- Marshes, ponds, oceans, or other bodies of water
- Wetlands
- Your neighbors' houses, depending on the size of the property
- Building and vegetative buffer setbacks required by zoning codes or homeowner covenants
- Bench mark elevation
- Base flood elevation
- North arrow and scale

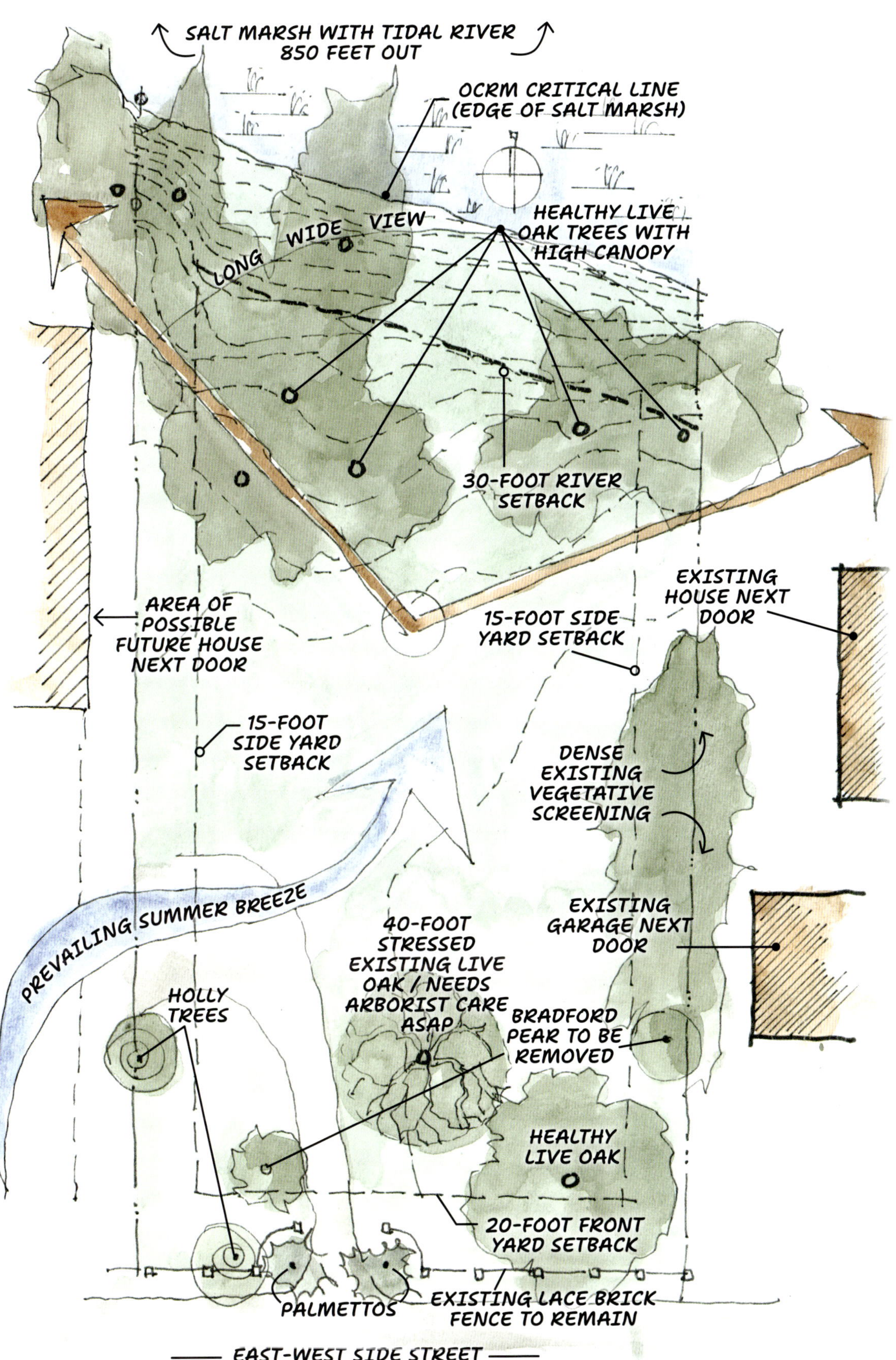
SALT MARSH WITH TIDAL RIVER
850 FEET OUT
OCRM CRITICAL LINE
(EDGE OF SALT MARSH)
LONG WIDE VIEW
HEALTHY LIVE
OAK TREES WITH
HIGH CANOPY
30-FOOT RIVER
SETBACK
EXISTING
HOUSE NEXT
DOOR
15-FOOT SIDE
YARD SETBACK
AREA OF
POSSIBLE
FUTURE HOUSE
NEXT DOOR
15-FOOT
SIDE YARD
SETBACK
DENSE
EXISTING
VEGETATIVE
SCREENING
EXISTING
GARAGE NEXT
DOOR
PREVAILING SUMMER BREEZE
40-FOOT
STRESSED
EXISTING LIVE
OAK / NEEDS
ARBORIST CARE
ASAP
HOLLY
TREES
BRADFORD
PEAR TO BE
REMOVED
HEALTHY
LIVE OAK
20-FOOT FRONT
YARD SETBACK
PALMETTOS
EXISTING LACE BRICK
FENCE TO REMAIN
EAST-WEST SIDE STREET

ABOVE: The tree limbs we designed the house around

OPPOSITE: This house was designed to curve around the live oak tree.

Site visits help us understand important details that aren't noted on the survey. Take a copy of your survey to the property and annotate the document with what you discover. Be sure to take photographs and note on the survey where you stood when the photo was taken. Also take some time to differentiate the good views from the bad. You'll use these notes to make sure the windows of your home are located in spots that will take advantage of the best views. These notes will also be useful when deciding where to place the roof and walls of the home and where driveways can be located to create a picturesque arrival experience.

Next, consider the site's natural surroundings, such as the tree canopies, the shape of the trees' limbs, and whether they wrap around one way or another. The trunk of a tree as located on the survey may not be a barrier to placing the home in a certain orientation—but the tree's *limbs* might be. For example, one house we designed was located on a tiny, quarter-acre lot on St. Simons Island, and it had an enormous tree. Fortunately, the tree was on the edge of the property. But we still had to work around both the footprint of the house and *the tree's limbs* to fit the house on the lot. The solution was to step the house back so that the limbs of the tree could float nicely *over* the house.

Sometimes trees can influence the shape of the home while also creating an interesting outdoor space. During one such project, we met with some clients after their real estate agents showed them three fairly small lots that they liked; the clients wanted to buy two of them. After studying the lots, it became clear which two lots were the best. However, a big live oak tree was situated between two of the lots. So we designed the front of their house to wrap around the tree, which resulted in a fabulous entry garden.

Microclimates

When you study the land, you will make some interesting discoveries about your property. Even though the South has a hot, humid climate, your site will have microclimates too. It's important to pay attention to those microclimates to see where you might locate inviting outdoor seating areas. In the right spot, these areas can be shaded by beautiful trees and cooled with prevailing breezes. We even use the homes we design to maximize favorable microclimates, as is the case with the dogtrot form.

The most important factor involved in designing a comfortable outdoor space is thermal comfort. Thermal comfort is a combination of air temperature, air motion, sunshine, and the temperature of surrounding surfaces. One of the ways Robert Marvin taught us to bring thermal comfort into landscape designs is by the introduction of little sun pockets in the garden. In the wintertime, a person could sit outside in front of a south-facing masonry wall that had soaked up the sun's heat while blocking the cold north wind. Achieving thermal comfort inside a home is also key for good health, well-being, and even productivity (we will cover this topic in chapter 6: "Systems").

Using the whole property is key to great home design. It's important to consider these unique microclimates on your site over the course of a day. Perhaps you'll want a special garden or garden room where you might want to go and sit by yourself, maybe on the eastern side of your property in the morning to drink your coffee. Even if your property isn't big, you can still create different opportunities to enjoy the different microclimates your property has to offer during the different seasons and times of day.

Sun Angles

The angles at which sunlight strikes a location on the earth's surface is ever-changing, seasonal, and very important to observe. In the South, it is important to minimize heat gain by minimizing the sun's angles into the home in the summer and maximizing them in the winter. The ideal orientation of a structure, therefore, is from east to west, where the northern and southern elevations are the longest side of the home. Northern light is ideal because it has no glare and minimal heat gain. It's relatively easy to protect a southern wall from direct sunlight with overhangs and porches, but it's harder to protect the east and west walls because of the sun's low angles.

The sun's angle on the west side of a home is particularly harsh because of the low, hot late-afternoon summer sun. By orienting a long, narrow home from east to west, with a porch on the south side, the sun is blocked from its most extreme heat. This design becomes a defense against any heat gain inside the home. When a home has its view to the west, we have to mitigate the harsh sun by introducing elements such as interior or exterior shades or louvers.

We work strategically with the sun's angles to understand how they will impact the home, and we use the Southern vernacular precedents to site it in order to keep it cool in summer and warm in winter. In doing so, the home will use much less electricity than it would otherwise. Getting to net zero is an important part of building sustainable, resilient homes. Net-zero homes minimize energy use, employing renewables and sustainable design to achieve a building that produces as much energy as it uses. This is a concept we will explore more in chapter 6: "Systems."

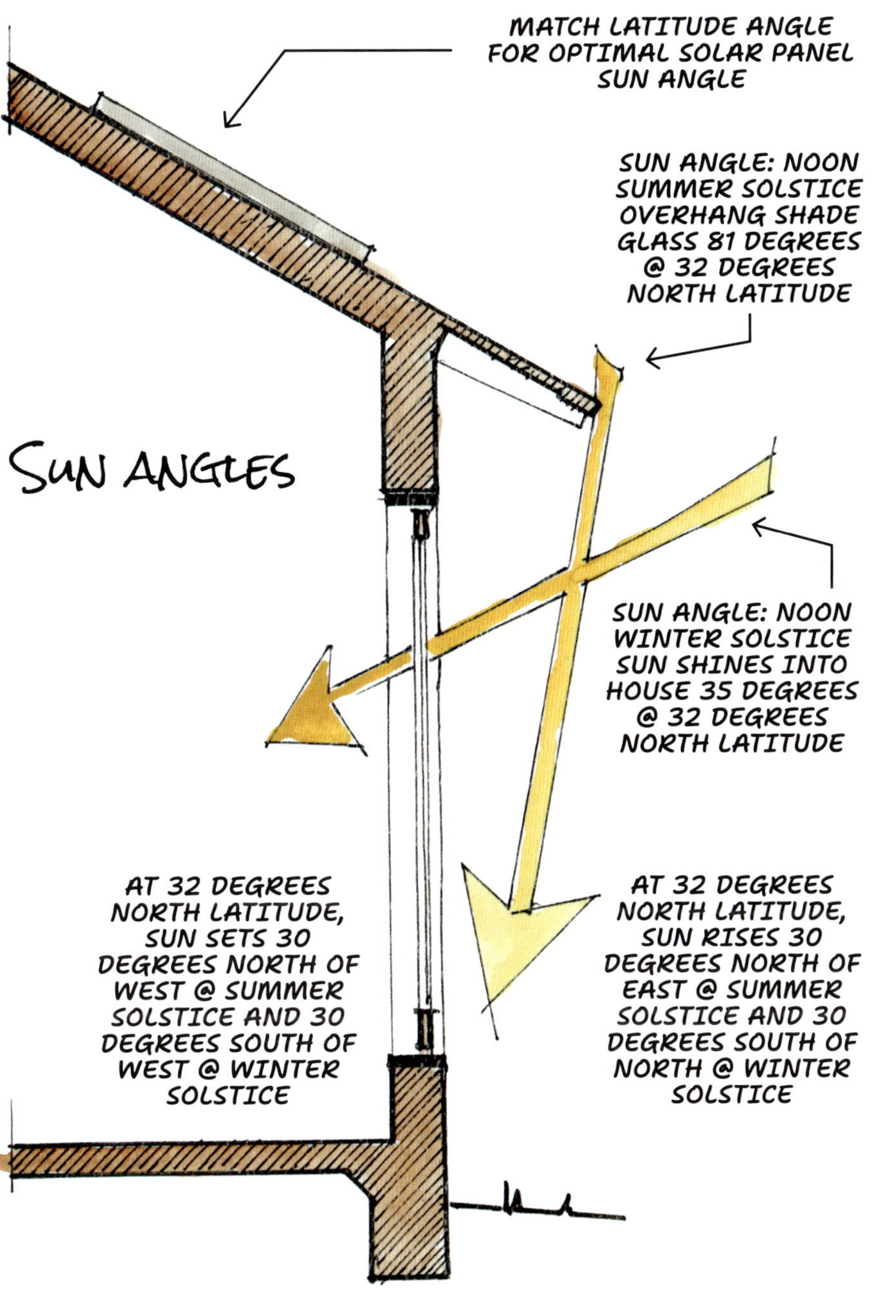
MATCH LATITUDE ANGLE
FOR OPTIMAL SOLAR PANEL
SUN ANGLE
SUN ANGLE: NOON
SUMMER SOLSTICE
OVERHANG SHADE
GLASS 81 DEGREES
@ 32 DEGREES
NORTH LATITUDE
SUN ANGLES
SUN ANGLE: NOON
WINTER SOLSTICE
SUN SHINES INTO
HOUSE 35 DEGREES
@ 32 DEGREES
NORTH LATITUDE
AT 32 DEGREES
NORTH LATITUDE,
SUN SETS 30
DEGREES NORTH OF
WEST @ SUMMER
SOLSTICE AND 30
DEGREES SOUTH OF
WEST @ WINTER
SOLSTICE
AT 32 DEGREES
NORTH LATITUDE,
SUN RISES 30
DEGREES NORTH OF
EAST @ SUMMER
SOLSTICE AND 30
DEGREES SOUTH OF
NORTH @ WINTER
SOLSTICE

Other Rules and Regulations

During a site study, there are several regulations to consider: building codes, which are typically adopted by the state but could also be by a municipality (most states have adopted the International Residential Code, with a few modifications); zoning ordinances established by the local jurisdiction; covenants or neighborhood design rules; and Federal Emergency Management Administration (FEMA) requirements if your property is in a designated floodplain.

Zoning

If you're buying a piece of property, it's important to understand your zoning regulations and those of your neighbors. Zoning is determined by your municipality or government jurisdiction, and it covers such things as what kind of buildings can be built on a property, how far you can build from the property line, the building size, lot coverage, how tall a building can be, and its uses. For example, some local people we know bought a home and were upset when, a year later, a huge apartment complex was built across the street from them (even though the project had been in the works for years). They could have discovered this by checking with the zoning department before they bought the property.

Many communities are adopting zoning ordinances that use the new urbanist gradient density—lots are zoned on a scale from total wilderness (where building is restricted entirely) to the densest urban area. Many

jurisdictions also have tree ordinances that determine which trees can and can't be cut down, depending on their size and species.

Zoning regulations also outline pervious to impervious ratios for the property specific to certain building materials. Impervious materials typically include everything under the roof in addition to the hardscape, such as driveways and terraces (green roofs and pervious pavers are an exception). These zoning regulations protect water quality and limit stormwater runoff.

Covenants

Typically, covenants are used in planned communities to determine the style and size of homes that can be built in the neighborhood, and also include a list of restrictions. Homeowners' associations usually have architectural review boards, typically composed of other homeowners who are tasked with reviewing a home's design for compliance with their adopted guidelines. Easements on properties usually grant someone or some entity the right to use a portion of another person's land or property. Utility companies needing to access sewer, gas, and plumbing equipment and driveway access for neighboring properties are examples of common easements. Verifying any easements on your site or covenants on the property you want to buy is equally as important as reviewing the zoning laws.

A few years ago, we were hired to design a home for a pie-shaped lot that had some strict covenants on it. It was a piece of property that their neighbor had decided to sell. The seller thought he'd put enough restrictions on the property to ensure that no one in the future could block his long river view. The covenant stated that only a one-story home could be built on the property. The site was located in a Historic Landmark District that required building heights to be within 10 percent of neighboring building heights. Often these kinds of lots can be purchased at a very reasonable price because of their "unbuildable" reputation.

The house that was built on the "unbuildable" lot

Instead of seeing limitations, good architects have an attitude that everything can be figured out and will begin putting together the pieces of the puzzle. In this case, the odd pie-shaped lot had a small buildable area. Due to the Historic Landmark District height regulation of being within 10 percent of the neighboring two-story houses, we were challenged to design a one-story house that had to be almost two stories high. Our solution was to raise the house up a full story above the floodplain. When we met with the building official, he agreed not to classify the part of the house located in the floodplain as the first story. Since we had some room to work with, we set the ceiling height at 14 feet, which met the height requirement required by the Historic Landmark District. We enjoyed putting those zoning, historic district guidelines, and covenant puzzle pieces together to create a beautiful home.

When a site challenge occurs due to a zoning ordinance, another option is to obtain a variance. A variance is a permission granted by a local zoning authority or board to deviate from the specific requirements of a zoning ordinance or regulation. However, variances to zoning ordinances can be difficult to get. Architects must go before a zoning variance board and make the case for why following the zoning ordinance would be a unique hardship for the owners of the property.

FEMA

The Federal Emergency Management Agency (FEMA) outlines important information to keep properties protected in the event of natural disasters. FEMA regulations regarding floodplains don't occur only along the coast; floodplains can be found along rivers, lakes, and other locations. Always check to see if your property is located in a flood hazard zone. Your surveyor will include the FEMA base flood elevation on the site survey. The base flood elevation (BFE) is the expected height of floodwaters during a base flood, which is defined as a flood that has a 1 percent chance of occurring in any given year. The BFE dictates the height that the first floor has to be above the ground. Your local jurisdiction will determine how high your first floor must be above the base flood elevation.

The only uses allowed in the floodplain are garages, storage rooms, and a staircase to the first floor. (If the building has an elevator, it can descend into the floodplain; when it is not in use, it must automatically return to the first story.) It's important to note that protection from flooding is a community effort. Everyone needs to adhere to the FEMA rules and regulations for storms. If they don't, noncompliance will be detrimental to the entire community. We will discuss more about these issues and how we saved a house by lifting it up out of a floodplain in the case study in chapter 7: "A Port in the Storm."

Septic Systems and Wells

In the best-case scenario, your property will be on a municipal water and sewer system. If the property does not have access, ask for a soil analysis test prior to buying the property, to make sure that septic is a viable option. A soil assessment, sometimes referred to as a percolation test, is a soil analysis method used to assess the rate at which water drains through the ground, typically conducted to determine the suitability of a site for installing a septic system. For example, it will indicate if you have a more pervious soil such as sand or rock, which is optimal for septic systems, as opposed to a more impervious kind of soil, such as clay. Likewise, if a property requires a well, it's important to make sure that it is also a viable option.

Some reasons a property might fail the soil assessment test include unacceptable soil conditions, a high water table, a too-small lot, or a location too close to an environmentally sensitive area. If the test fails, there are some alternative on-site engineered options, but they can be expensive and too complicated for residential use.

Knowing what the regulations are for septic systems and wells is a very important aspect of due diligence when purchasing a property. When one of our clients needed to find the location for their septic tank and field, it led to a very challenging situation. They already owned a piece of property when we met them. The health department rules dictated that septic systems needed to be at least 50 feet away from a well (i.e., a setback). Each of their neighbors had a well almost on the property line. There was no place on their property to put the septic field because they couldn't meet the 50-foot setback. In order to install their septic system, they had to pay for the installation of a new well for their neighbor.

Courtesy of Eric Horan

Riparian Buffers

When we first moved to Beaufort, there were no river setbacks, so people could build right up to the edge of the water. It's a natural tendency, since people love the water. (However, there are unforeseen consequences of building too close to the water—one of which we couldn't have anticipated. It was the early '90s, and a contractor was digging the foundation for a project. Each night, a little alligator would climb into its foundation. And every day, the contractors had to wrestle this 3-foot alligator out of the foundation, until they eventually poured the concrete.)

Over time, scientists began to realize how this practice of constructing homes at the water's edge adversely affected our water quality. That's when riparian buffers became the norm.

A riparian buffer refers to the land that borders waterways; it's characterized by a cover of native vegetation consisting of trees, shrubs, and grasses. The benefits of riparian buffers include preventing erosion, abating flood and storm damage, providing wildlife habitat, improving aesthetics of water corridors (which can increase property values), and maintaining and improving water quality and overall health of the ecosystem by filtering pollutants from runoff. According to the Environmental Protection Agency (EPA), riparian buffers "act as natural filters of source pollutants, including sediment, nutrients, pathogens, and metals to water bodies." People on the river experience another advantage of these buffers when they look back at the land. Instead of seeing house after house lining the waterfront, they see some beautiful natural landscape.

All photographs in this case study courtesy of John McManus

CASE STUDY:
RIVERFRONT HOME

Our clients desired a sustainable retreat that maximized the views on their riverfront lot. This is a true dogtrot, with an open space separating the primary suite from the public rooms. The dogtrot serves as the foyer and a sitting area. A perforated wall and door on the front and a folding perforated wall on the rear can be closed and locked for security. The dogtrot was oriented to capture the prevailing breezes off the river and over the swimming pool. When the house was under construction, the contractors set up their staging in the dogtrot to take advantage of the breeze.

Comfortable, outdoor living areas also reduce the amount of air-conditioned space needed in the house. A light-filled great room has operable windows and transoms for great cross ventilation. South-facing windows were protected by a large overhang designed to block the summer sun and allow the winter sun to fill the great room. Folding walls help the house seamlessly transition from inside to outside.

The outdoor living space has motorized retractable screens set at an angle to the main house for a long view down the river. A lap pool and spa are centered on the entry, which immediately connects one to the view of the river. A large terrace curves around a live oak tree. Meanwhile, a boardwalk encircles the outdoor terrace to break up the grade, which eliminates the need for guardrails.

Other sustainable strategies include a reflective "cool roof," cypress reverse board-and-batten siding, river-recovered cypress ceilings, spectrally selective glass in impact-resistant windows and doors, cellulose foam insulation, a conditioned crawl space, reclaimed heart pine floors, a super-high-efficiency heat pump with an energy recovery ventilator, and low-VOC (volatile organic compound) paint and finishes.

Riverfront Home: Sustainable Strategies

VERNACULAR

- Dogtrot
- One room wide
- Long east–west axis
- Oriented to capture breezes
- High ceilings
- Large overhangs to block summer sun
- South-facing porches

CONTEMPORARY

- Reversed board and batten
- Large outdoor living
- Local cypress siding
- Local cypress ceilings
- Conditioned attics and crawl space
- VOC-free paint
- Formaldehyde-free cabinetry
- High-performance heat pump with ERV
- Reflective "cool roof" metal roof
- Reclaimed heart pine floor
- Blower door test
- Impact-rated, aluminum-clad wood casement windows with spectrally selective glass
- High windows on north side to flood interior with light
- Limited lawn
- Sited to protect existing trees
- Native landscaping

Project Completed: 2008

Builder: Brunson Construction
Hampton, South Carolina

SECTION II:

The ART and SCIENCE of Sustainability

CHAPTER 3
Connecting with the Land

"We will never be truly healthy, satisfied, or fulfilled if we live apart and alienated from the environment from which we evolved."

—Stephen R. Kellert, professor emeritus of social ecology and senior research scholar at the Yale University School of Forestry and Environmental Studies

Senegalese forestry engineer Baba Dioum once said, "In the end, we conserve only what we love, we will love only what we understand, and we will understand only what we are taught." This profound connection between love, understanding, and conservation suggests that we nurture and support what we truly care about. Making these connections with our clients and learning what they care about is our focus at the beginning of any project.

We believe that the art of sustainability lies in design. When we design a beautiful home, it naturally becomes more resilient. Our design process begins with the site study, which helps us decide where each activity in the home should occur on the property. For example, we consider where the owners will most enjoy the outdoors and how contractors can best access the property during construction. We then combine the site study with the clients' program—an inventory we make with them at the beginning of the project that lists what they want and need in their home based on their lifestyle. The list includes the desired number of bedrooms and baths and any other living spaces they require. The site study, together with the clients' program, often generates the big concepts of the design, which gives the entire process a clear direction that determines all future design decisions.

Our process continues as we synthesize the information from the site study, the clients' program, and the lessons learned from vernacular precedents to properly site the home. For example, if we have a beautiful tree on the property, our concept might be to design all the rooms to have a view of that tree. Alternatively, if the client doesn't have a view, the concept might be to turn inward to create views.

Great home design is site and client specific; it occurs in the sweet spot where the clients' requirements combine with the best use of the site. The sketch design is the first visual generation of our concept and includes a floor plan on the site study and sketches of the exterior. Deeper design discussions begin when we present these first sketches to our clients. The analysis of the site's attributes combines with the owners' program and concept to create a path forward to complete the design of the home and its environs.

A principal consideration is how our clients will enter and experience their property. The site design creates a progression from public space to increasingly private spaces. This public-to-private journey begins when you leave the street. Imagine driving up to your home—you leave the public world behind and descend into your own private world. It's important to design the approach to a home so that it has an air of mystery and adventure. For example, perhaps the driveway passes under leafy trees that frame a gateway into your private sanctuary. Different patterns on the driveway could invite you to cross the threshold from the outside world into the personal. Providing a few episodic moments upon arrival helps connect our clients and their guests to the property.

We aim to draw people to their homes in ways that reflect each client's personality, creating a unique, tailored experience. For example, you may want your guests to walk to the front door and immediately see the home's

The view to the Zen garden is revealed when you walk into our office conference room. *Courtesy of Kim Smith*

Courtesy of Kim Smith

beautiful view. Or perhaps, those guests will have just a peek of a view before entering the home, to be surprised by a captured view. We also use these views to entice our clients and their guests to outdoor living areas.

In the South, we extend our living spaces outside. Outdoor rooms are a cost-effective way to build that also ties homeowners to nature. To create outdoor rooms (and save trees), we often position separate smaller buildings on a property. By designing a home with smaller buildings instead of one large structure, it can often be located among mature trees and look like it has been on the property forever. Breaking up a home into several buildings—a separate garage, guesthouse, and the main house, for example—also creates opportunities for outdoor living areas between the buildings.

We draw on the lessons learned from the vernacular precedents in determining how we might arrange separate buildings in relation to the prevailing winds, the best views, and the surrounding trees to create more sustainable, healthier homes with dynamic outdoor spaces. The ideal design solution will have the long axis of the building running east to west to minimize heat gain and glare. Beyond comfort, natural, and aesthetic considerations, having separate buildings on a site brings other important benefits. For example, designing garages to be disconnected from the main home protects owners from carbon monoxide fumes and fire hazards. By carefully positioning multiple buildings, we can also avoid damaging the native trees and understory vegetation.

In this chapter, we will examine our connection to the land, how we and our homes connect to our sites, and why that connection is important. Many site-specific topics will be illuminated, such as how to respect the site by protecting trees, addressing stormwater runoff, and leveraging the native landscape. In this chapter's case study, "Building the Unbuildable," we will talk more about how to work around site obstacles—whether human-made (e.g., HOA restrictions) or natural (e.g., trees).

ABOVE: *Courtesy of John McManus*

OPPOSITE: This house takes advantage of the small side yard for an outdoor living space. *Courtesy of Kim Smith*

Site Size

We enjoy the process of designing homes that reflect the unique aspects of every property. Large lots of several acres afford many options to orient the home, while home placement is most limited in a neighborhood with small lots.

When designing homes in neighborhoods, the challenge is often the competing desires of connecting to the land while also maintaining privacy from nearby neighbors. Often, the solution is to create an inward-looking view of your property through courtyards, water features, and landscaped rooms. Water features can provide a place of calm meditation within a garden or courtyard, while its bubbling sound can mask neighborhood noise. Planting a vegetative screen can enhance the privacy of an outdoor living space and make it feel more like a retreat and less exposed.

In addition to site consideration, the home design needs to be thought of on a larger scale, in relation to the surrounding area. We once had a client contact us because they wanted to make sure that a lot was buildable. They were concerned because the client's twin sister lived next door; when they built their home, they didn't want to block the sister's beautiful marsh view. So we intentionally set the house on the lot in a way that protected the sister's view.

This brings up an important point about designing a home that sits on a property adjacent to a vacant lot. In such a case, we try to envision where a future owner might put a house on that lot. We do an analysis of the site to consider where their views are and where they might put their outdoor spaces, so that we can respect the future use of the land and protect our client's privacy.

How to Respect the Site

When designing your home, it's important to respect the site. Each piece of land has its own unique characteristics. From the topography to native vegetation, many factors play a vital role in shaping the aesthetic and functional aspects of the design. By embracing and integrating these site-specific elements, the home not only becomes a thing of beauty but also fosters a sustainable and enduring relationship between the architecture and the environment.

Tree Protection

Beyond saving trees because of their natural beauty, protecting trees during home construction is crucial for ecological balance and environmental health. Trees provide oxygen, absorb carbon dioxide (also known as sequestering carbon), offer shade, absorb stormwater

runoff through their root system, and support biodiversity by providing animal habitats.

> Average interception of rainfall by a forest canopy ranges from 10–40 percent depending on species, time of year, and precipitation rates per storm event. In urban and suburban settings, a single deciduous tree can intercept from 500 to 760 gallons per year; and a mature evergreen can intercept more than 4,000 gallons per year. . . .
>
> One Forest Service Researcher has stated that planting large canopy trees over impervious surfaces, such as a parking lot or street, has much greater impact on reducing stormwater (up to eight times greater) because it works to reduce peak flows in urban settings. ("The Role of Trees and Forests in Healthy Watersheds" by Vincent Cotrone, extension.psu.edu)

Preserving mature trees also enhances property value, reduces energy costs, and contributes to a sustainable and aesthetically pleasing environment that benefits not only us but also the broader ecosystem. Also, it's important to add trees to your site whenever possible. Green spaces soak up pollution and cool heated spaces.

> Plants, especially woody plants, are very good at removing . . . contaminants (such as metals, pesticides, solvents, oils, and hydrocarbons) from soil and water. These pollutants are either used for growth (nutrients) or are stored in wood. In one study, a single sugar maple growing roadside removed 60mg of cadmium, 140mg of chromium, 820mg of nickel, and 5200mg of lead in a single growing season. ("The Role of Trees and Forests in Healthy Watersheds" by Vincent Cotrone, extension.psu.edu)

The site study identifies parts of the property that need to be protected. An important preconstruction activity is installing tree protection fencing and silt fencing to minimize erosion and runoff. The tree protection fences are ideally placed at the trees' drip line (where their canopies end) so that the roots aren't compacted by construction activity. We specify wooden split-rail fencing for tree protection. The fencing provides good, sustainable protection because it is not easily knocked over and the contractor can reuse it on the next job.

Once we understand the areas of the site that need protection, we create a mobilization plan that specifies how contractors can access the site, where they can put their building materials, and what areas will be used for dumpsters and port-a-potties.

SUSTAINABLE IMPACTS OF TREES

- A large oak tree can consume about 100 gallons of water per day, and a giant sequoia can drink up to 500 gallons daily—but even a single small tree can make big differences; some can absorb as much as 58 gallons of stormwater from a ½-inch rain event.
- Trees help us breathe . . . yet, even without the oxygen, trees clearly offer plenty of other benefits, from food, medicine, and raw materials to shade, windbreaks, and flood control.
- Adding one tree to an open pasture can increase its bird biodiversity from almost zero species to as high as eighty.
- Trees can lower stress, raise property values, and fight crime—landscaping with healthy, mature trees adds an average of 10 percent to a property's value (some estimates are as high as 20 percent). Research also shows that urban trees are correlated with lower rates of crimes, including activities ranging from graffiti, vandalism, and littering to domestic violence.
- A large oak tree can drop 10,000 acorns in one year—while most of those may end up as a meal for birds and mammals, every so often a lucky acorn gets started on a journey that will carry it hundreds of feet into the sky and a century into the future.

—From "15 Astounding Facts About Trees" by Russell McLendon, treehugger.com, and "The Role of Trees and Forests in Healthy Watersheds" by Vincent Cotrone, extension.psu.edu

Stormwater

It's important to contain the stormwater runoff on your property so that it doesn't pollute a river, an ocean, a lake, or your neighbor's yard. The Environmental Protection Agency (EPA) outlines how stormwater is a source of pollutants: "Stormwater runoff can pick up and deposit harmful pollutants like trash, chemicals, and dirt/sediments into streams, lakes and groundwater from construction sites, lawns, and improperly stored hazardous wastes."

Stormwater runoff can be mitigated with a variety of methods, including collecting the water from your roof in a cistern or a rain barrel. The advantage of using a cistern or a rain barrel is that the water is reclaimed for irrigation and other nonpotable uses.

A more beautiful solution is to manipulate the topographical surface to create a rain garden. Rain gardens pool the water runoff, turning it into a pond where native wetland plants can grow. When dry, the feature becomes a rock garden; when it rains, it turns into a lush water feature that filters the water as it slowly seeps back into the aquifer. Using reclaimed rainwater to irrigate the landscape is more sustainable than using treated water and is more nutrient-rich too.

The rain garden in the foreground is planted with native species. *Courtesy of John McManus*

Native Landscaping

Preserving existing native plants is important from a sustainability and resiliency point of view. Using native plants respects the land. When landscaping with them—instead of clearing the land and planting a large lawn, for instance—you will have a smaller carbon footprint. Working with native plants is a way of respecting the whole ecosystem so that we avoid creating a monoculture. Through plant selection, we can encourage the diverse local wildlife and pollinators to inhabit the land. Landscaping with native plants fosters a thriving ecosystem by providing a familiar and supportive habitat for local wildlife species. These plants thrive in the region's climate and soil conditions and attract a diverse range of insects, birds, and other wildlife, promoting biodiversity and ecological balance. It's a thrill to look out the window and see hummingbirds and butterflies in our garden of native species.

We have dedicated our careers to combining contemporary building science with the lessons learned from the Southern vernacular precedents. We have shown how we use the vernacular precedents as inspiration for both the building and site designs. Once we've sited the home, we detail it with the most current building science and sustainability methods. Current building science for hot, humid climates demands a tight building enclosure, which we will explore in the next chapter.

Landscaping with native plants requires fewer resources and supports the local wildlife.

CASE STUDY:
BUILDING THE UNBUILDABLE

Clients frequently seek our advice about which properties to buy. When we first consulted with our clients in this case study, they wanted us to look at land that was considered unbuildable because so many large trees were located in the middle of the small lot. They asked our opinion about whether they would be able to build a home on the site and still preserve the trees. In this case, we were able to assure them that they could build the house they desired and save the mature live oaks.

The property was the last waterfront lot in a development, and it was covered with beautiful, mature live oak trees. It also had really long, wonderful views down a wide tidal creek. When we toured the site with the clients, we figured out how to slide their home among the trees on the property without having to cut down any of the trees. To do this, we had to request a small variance for the setback of the home from the HOA, which was granted.

The home design was V shaped; it folded around some of the big trees, giving our clients water views from almost every room in their home. With a long east-to-west axis, the home had windows that could be opened to catch the river breezes, while also providing our clients with minimal heat gain and glare. Overhangs were sized to block the summer sun and invite the winter sun into the great room. The water side of the house faced north, which was perfect for its big windows. The canted outdoor living space took advantage of the prevailing breezes. A long porch ran the length of the 4,000-square-foot home, where our clients enjoyed outdoor living and the occasional sighting of dolphins, sea otters, and manatees. We built the structure 15 feet above the creek to prevent flooding.

The clients purchased the lot at a pretty good price because of its "unbuildable" reputation. They have since received a rich return on their investment.

Building the Unbuildable: Sustainable Strategies

VERNACULAR

- Long east–west axis
- Large overhangs
- Oriented to capture prevailing breezes
- Tall ceilings
- Porch on south side
- Extensive glazing on north side

CONTEMPORARY

- Conditioned attic
- Drainage plane
- Cedar shingles
- Impact wood clad casement windows with SHGC of 0.19, Energy Star certified
- Formaldehyde-free cabinets
- VOC-free paints and coatings
- High-efficiency heat pump with ERV
- Cypress ceiling
- Blower door test
- Minimal lawn
- LED lights
- Native landscape on waterside

Project Completed: 2016

Builder: Cameron & Cameron
Hilton Head Island, South Carolina

Courtesy of Jeff Amberg

CHAPTER 4
Building Enclosures

"Building houses is really about the durability of people, which is their health, safety and welfare; the durability of the building, which is the useful service life of a building. And it's typically limited by its durability and the durability of the planet, which is the well-being of the local and global environment."

—Joe Lstiburek, PhD, P.Eng., ASHRAE Fellow

"All buildings should have firmitas, utilitas, et venustas (firmness, commodity, and delight)."

—Vitruvius, 1 BCE

Seasonal variations in the South play a significant role when designing for sustainability. While winters here tend to be mild, summers bring intense heat waves and the potential for severe storms—this is our hot and humid climate. A hot, humid region is defined as a place that receives more than 20 inches of annual precipitation and where the average monthly temperature remains above 45 degrees Fahrenheit throughout the year. During the summer months, temperatures in the southern United States can soar well into the 90s, and annual precipitation hovers around 50 inches. The hot, humid air in the South carries a substantial amount of water vapor, giving it a muggy, sticky feel, which can intensify the perception of already high temperatures.

As we have explored earlier, this combination of high temperatures and humidity poses a number of challenges for home design. The most important challenge we face is how to effectively seal a home from the elements while still introducing fresh air inside. The three major changes over the past fifty years—air-conditioning, tighter building enclosures, and thermal insulation—have brought much-needed benefits and greater comfort to our homes. However, other challenges, such as mold and mildew, arose from inadequate home construction (albeit unintentionally so). This was often the result of inappropriate materials that were also (many times) improperly installed.

In this chapter, we will review the techniques and best practices used today to appropriately build in a hot, humid climate. We begin by discussing the roots of most degradation problems: moisture and its various sources. We then delve into the building enclosure and how it manages the flow of moisture, air, and heat. A lot of the information we share has to do with preventing water damage and the resulting mold, mildew, and termites that can follow. We'll conclude with our case study, "More Than an Addition."

Moisture

As we discovered early in our building science journey, moisture is the root of almost all problems when it comes to the degradation of a building. Joe Lstiburek once said that the single most important factor affecting the durability of a building is the deterioration of its materials by moisture. The best defense for water problems is to manage it at the source, which can be from either the outside or the inside of a building. The following are the most common water sources that can cause home damage.

Rainwater

We have lots of rain in the South, which means water infiltration is more likely. Therefore, we need more rain controls than is needed in homes in drier climates. The water control layer is the first defense to keep rainwater out; this includes proper flashing, drainage planes, and exterior siding. Large roof overhangs can shield the exterior wall, which helps it stay dry. (Gable roofs without overhangs should be avoided due to the amount of rainfall in the region.) If you desire a flat roof, an overhang should still be incorporated into the design. Gutters and downspouts should direct the water away from the house. The grade also needs to slope away from the house, in order to prevent moisture from entering the crawl space.

Groundwater

If your home has a crawl space (we discuss crawl spaces in detail later in the chapter), a vapor retarder is necessary to prevent moisture from migrating from the ground into the crawl space. If the water table is high, a foundation drain—a trench filled with gravel or rock containing a perforated pipe—may be needed. The pipe redirects surface water and prevents groundwater accumulation by facilitating drainage away from a specific area; it's commonly used to prevent basement flooding or to manage water runoff in landscaping. (Due to high water tables and a lack of a deep frost line, most houses in the Coastal South do not have basements.)

The inside of the wall that started our building science journey

Courtesy of
John McManus

Plumbing Leaks

There are many places in the home where plumbing leaks can occur, causing significant damage in a short amount of time. The best practice is not to install a water heater in an attic, where a leak could cause significant issues. It is also prudent to install drain pans and water-resistant flooring in rooms with washing machines and water heaters (drain pans should be piped to the exterior). An audible alarm can help detect a leak in the water heater.

Heat pumps pull a lot of moisture from the interior of your house, and clogged condensation drains from the interior air handler can also cause major leakages. Most heat pump units will recognize when the drain is clogged and will shut off automatically—but not always.

This range hood makes a statement with the antique mirror. *Courtesy of Kim Smith*

Indoor Water Vapor

Indoor water vapor refers to water generally produced by cooking, showering, and even breathing. A good ventilation hood above the kitchen cooktop (a quiet one is preferable so that you will actually use it) and exhaust bathroom fans tied to an occupancy sensor (runs for a set amount of time) can prevent trapping water vapor indoors.

Moist Outdoor Air

When moist outdoor air enters a building, it interacts with the cold air inside, and this can cause condensation to pool on surfaces, which in turn can host mold and mildew. We talk about how to prevent this problem in "Air Control Layer" in the next section.

Building Enclosures

The most basic purpose of a building is to shelter us from the environment. That is why the building enclosure is so important. The building enclosure refers to the elements of a building that separate the outside unconditioned environment from the conditioned inside—its roof, doors, windows, floors, and walls, for example. This boundary regulates the flow of moisture, air, and heat in and out of the structure. The various components of the building enclosure work together to provide thermal comfort, energy efficiency, and protection against the elements.

The building enclosure has three control layers in hot, humid climates:

- The first layer guards against liquid water with a water control layer and flashing.
- The second layer is the air control barrier, which seals the enclosure from air.
- The third layer is the thermal control barrier of insulation.

It is essential that these control layers are continuous to properly manage the passage of water, air, and heat. If there are gaps or holes, problems such as mold, mildew, and vermin can occur. In the following sections, we will discuss these three control layers and why the fourth control layer, the vapor barrier, is not used in hot, humid climates.

Water Control Layer

The one constant in hot, humid climates is that the building will get wet. The walls have to have a way to dry in order to minimize the amount of water that could enter the building. Therefore, the water control layer, which controls liquid water, is especially important.

The water control layer is composed of a water barrier, flashing, and other liquid management details on the exterior of the house. Joe Lstiburek explained the objective of the water control layer in this way: "The fundamental principle of water management is to shed water by layering materials in such a way that water is directed downwards and outwards of the building or away from the building."

Since we know that the wall is going to get wet, we need to take additional steps to allow it to dry. The best building practice is to have an air gap of at least 1/8 inch between a wall's water control layer and the exterior cladding. This drainage space creates a capillary break that draws off water and allows it to evaporate or drain to the exterior.

Flashing is another integral part of the water control layer because it prevents water penetration at intersections and joints in a building enclosure, such as around windows and doors and the transitions where a roof meets a wall or chimney.

Air Control Layer

Over the years, many contractors have argued that houses need to breathe—there must be fresh air in the house to prevent indoor air pollution. The fallacy of this argument is best refuted by Allison A. Bailes in his book *A House Needs to Breathe . . . or Does It?*:

> "If a leaky house is the solution . . . how does that work? Those random holes are going to bring air into the house from places like the smelly garage, the moldy crawl space and the dirty attic. . . . We understand this now. Random leaks don't bring in fresh air, so we seal up the house and make sure it is airtight as possible and then intentionally bring in air from a location where we know it will be as fresh as possible."

According to the Department of Energy (DOE), the leaks of a leaky house can account for 30 percent or more of a home's heating and cooling costs. Adding an air control layer blocks air from leaking in or out of the house. The air control layer is a combination of an air barrier, such as a house wrap, and sealing holes with caulk, gaskets, tape, and foam sealants. In hot, humid climates, the air barrier should be located on the exterior side of the sheathing. Depending on the products used, the water control layer and the air control layer can be the same layer.

Identifying and sealing air gaps is essential in creating a tight enclosure. Air gaps are often found around plumbing chases, around windows and doors, at the intersections of roof and walls, in eaves, and near

vents and electrical connections. To help identify any holes or gaps in the air barrier, conduct a blower door test prior to the installation of insulation or finishes.

The blower door test serves as a diagnostic tool to find air leaks so that they can be sealed. The test involves closing all openings in a building's enclosure—doors, windows, and dampers—and then using a powerful fan mounted in an exterior doorway to depressurize the interior. By controlling the pressure difference between the inside and outside of the building, the blower door test can measure the air infiltration rate. An additional blower door test is often conducted after the interior wall finish is installed. This ensures that the air control layer was not compromised while the mechanical, plumbing, and electrical rough-ins were installed.

The standard pressure difference is 50 pascals, which is the pressure a 20 mph wind would create. The blower door test result number represents the amount of air changes that occur in a house per hour at 50 pascals (ACH50). The 2021 International Energy Conservation Code (IECC) mandates a blower door test result of 3.0 (ACH50 or below), or three air changes per hour. We aim for fewer than two air changes (ACH50) in our projects. The lower the number of air changes, the tighter the building enclosure.

One of the most important aspects of constructing tighter buildings for the hot, humid climate is the implementation of systems that bring in fresh air for the health of the occupants. We use an energy recovery ventilator (ERV) to introduce fresh air into the homes we design; this removes both heat and moisture from the air brought into the house. (We will discuss ERVs in more detail in chapter 6: "Systems.")

The building is set up for a blower door test.
Courtesy of Elm Energy Group

Thermal Control Layer

The second law of thermodynamics states that heat always travels from hot to cold by one of three means: conduction, convection, or radiation. Conduction occurs when heat travels directly through a material that is controlled by insulation. Convection occurs when heat is transferred by another medium, such as air. Radiation refers to the absorption of heat from a heat source; in

our case, the sun. (We will discuss this more in the section on windows in this chapter.)

Insulation and assemblies (such as walls and roofs) are measured in R-values, which is the thermal resistance or the ability of a material to resist the flow of heat. The higher the R-value, the better the material insulates. It is important to note the difference between the R-value of a material and the R-value of an assembly. In a house, about 20 percent of the wall is the structure, sheathing, windows, doors, and interior and exterior finishes. If the insulation in the wall has an R-value of R-15, then the overall R-value for the wall assembly might be around R-9. The lower R-value occurs because the combination of the materials of the wall—sheathing, studs, etc.—with the insulation is less than the R-value of the insulation.

Understanding the numerous types of insulation used for different applications can be a bit overwhelming. Building Green, an organization dedicated to sustainable design and building, researched the existing options for insulation and rated the different types of insulation by the amount of recycled content, embodied energy, and toxic emission emitted throughout its life, as well as the amount of toxic emissions created during manufacturing and installation. For residential use, they recommend dense-packed cellulose or spray-applied fiberglass for above-grade walls and roofs, polyisocyanurate for basements and crawl space walls, and mineral wool for slab edges.

We prefer spray-applied fiberglass for the walls and roofs in our hot, humid climate, because if the cellulose insulation gets wet, it doesn't dry easily. Spray-foam insulation is very effective at insulation, and it provides an excellent air barrier. However, there are health and environmental concerns with spray-foam insulation; therefore, it is not recommended by Building Green. (We will write more about the health implications of the materials used in home design in the next chapter, Materials for Health, Durability & Aesthetics.)

How much insulation is enough? Building Green and the DOE recommend the following insulation for our hot, humid climate.

Slabs	R-0
Basement walls or crawl space walls	R-10
Floors above a vented crawl space	R-15
Walls above grade	R-15
Roofs	R-40

One concern when building in colder climates is thermal bridging. This occurs when there is a direct connection between the outside and the inside, which causes heat to move unimpeded, such as at the attachment of wood sheathing to the wood studs. The solution is continuous insulation, and this is usually installed on the exterior. Of course, we are building in a hot and humid climate. In the Coastal South, the 2021 IECC (International Energy Conservation Code) does not require continuous insulation to prevent thermal bridging. We have learned that continuous insulation and exceeding the recommended insulation values cited in the chart above have a diminishing return on investment. Your money is better spent on high-quality windows.

Vapor Control Layer

Historically, when all building codes were written for cold climates, vapor barriers were required behind the interior wall finish for when the warm inside air would drive moisture outward in the wintertime. But in a hot, humid climate, this also meant that in the summer the vapor barrier would cause surface condensation to occur in the wall's interior cavity, leading to mold and mildew. Exterior walls in hot, humid climates must be able to dry both to the interior and exterior; this is why we do not use vapor barriers. The best way to control vapor transmission in hot, humid climates is through the air and moisture control layers and a drainage space. (And vinyl wallpaper should not be used in hot, humid climates because it creates a decorative vapor barrier that will cause mold and mildew to grow.)

Doors and Windows

Glass doors and windows are the weakest links for heat flow and may be the most challenging—and most important—component of the building enclosure. As Corey Squire, architect and nationally recognized expert in sustainable design, writes in his book *People, Planet, Design*:

> Everything important in a building comes down to its windows. Daylighting depends on windows, as do thermal comfort, views, energy performances and so many other outcomes that we care about. Because of their pivotal role and sheer impact, windows are always the first place to invest resources for all-around better outcomes.

A building is an integrated system, and this includes our window placement and glazing strategies. A good rule of thumb is to limit the glass-to-solid-wall ratio for houses to 30 percent. If a house has a long axis running east to west, we can locate the majority of the windows on the north and south sides, where it is easy to control both heat gain and glare. We then limit windows on the east and west. Swing windows, casements, awnings, or European tilt/turn windows generally perform better over the long term because the sash compresses the air seal when it is closed and locked.

Always purchase the highest-performing windows available. A code-minimum solid wall is roughly six times more thermally resistive than a code-minimum window; therefore, upping the performance of the window will increase the effective R-value for the entire wall assembly.

Window performance is measured in several factors: the U-factor, the solar heat gain coefficient (SHGC), air leakage, and the design pressure (DP). The U-factor represents the thermal transmittance and effectiveness as an insulator. A lower U-factor indicates better insulation and reduced heat transfer. This keeps heat inside during cold weather and outside during hot weather. While a lower U-factor is helpful in any climate, it is more critical in a cold climate. In a hot, humid climate, the recommended U-factor value is 0.35 or less.

The more important performance criterion in a hot, humid climate is the SHGC, which is defined by the DOE as "the fraction of solar radiation admitted through a window, door, or skylight and released as heat inside the building." The SHGC is a number between 0 and 1, where a lower SHGC number indicates less solar heat gain and better shading ability. In the South, you want a SHGC of 0.25 or less. Energy-efficient windows have spectrally selective glass that is designed to control the SHGC while allowing visible light to pass through.

Air leakage is defined by the DOE as "the rate of air movement around a door, window, or skylight in the presence of a specific pressure difference across it. It's expressed in units of cubic feet per minute per square foot of frame area (cfm/ft_2)." The best possible air leakage value is 0.1 cfm/ft_2. When selecting windows for a hot, humid climate, make sure the value is below 0.3 cfm/ft_2 and preferably below 0.2 cfm/ft_2.

The DP rating indicates the amount of pressure a window or door can withstand from wind, water, or a structural load without breaking. The required DP rating is calculated using the design wind speed for a particular location, orientation, and placement on the facade. A higher DP number represents a stronger window. The International Residential Code (IRC) defines where DP-rated products are required in the building. Windows or doors located within 4 feet of the edge of a building require a higher DP rating.

Window frames are even worse for heat leakage performance than the glass. To minimize the negative effect, choose clad wood or fiberglass window frames. Avoid solid metal frames; they transfer heat easily, even if they are thermally broken (a design that separates the interior and exterior sections of the frame to minimize the transfer of heat or cold). Using a few larger windows, instead of many smaller windows, will lessen the negative effect because there are fewer frames.

Finally, we recommend that all of our clients invest in impact windows and doors. Impact windows, also known as hurricane windows, are specially designed to withstand the impact of flying debris and high winds associated with severe weather conditions such as hurricanes or tropical storms. Impact windows also offer excellent noise reduction.

Building Enclosure Components—Foundations

Now that we have covered the basics of the water, air, and thermal control layers, let's examine some particular applications in the home, starting with foundations. There are generally two types of foundations: concrete slabs on grade and crawl spaces. Basements are unusual in the South due to the high water table. There is no need for the footings to be below a frost line, so it is not cost effective to dig a basement in hot, humid climates.

Concrete Slabs on Grade

A concrete slab on grade, or raised above the existing grade on fill, needs all three of the control layers used in the South—water, air, and thermal. The water and air barriers are most important because concrete is porous—it will pull water out of the ground. The moisture and air barrier has three elements:

- A layer of gravel
- A layer of polyethylene, 10 to 15 mils thick
- Sealing at every penetration with the appropriate tape or sealant

The slab will also need to be air-sealed at the intersection of the slab and wall.

The thermal insulation layer is provided by a perimeter of rigid insulation. The 2021 IECC exempts this insulation in jurisdictions designated as prone to a heavy termite infestation. Green Building recommends mineral wool because it is termite resistant, and this is also what we specify.

Crawl Spaces

Crawl spaces can either be open or enclosed. Open crawl spaces are often located on piers or pilings with no foundation walls. They are also typically found wherever a house has been built above the base flood elevation and breakaway walls are required because it is located in a V flood zone (V stands for velocity and is usually on oceanfront property). In this instance, the water, air, and thermal control layers are at the underside of the first floor.

Enclosed crawl spaces have continuous foundation walls. Historically, these were vented. A vented crawl space in a hot, humid climate would cause a major problem. The hot, humid air in the crawl space would leak through the openings cut in the floor for plumbing and ductwork, creating condensation as it mixed with the cool inside air, creating mold and mildew.

The preferred method is to encapsulate, or seal, the crawl space and add conditioned air. In this way, the water, air, and thermal control layers are located at the crawl space floor and walls. We typically add a thin, 2-inch slab with the control layers as detailed for a slab. The IRC also allows a layer of 10-mil polyethylene on the ground instead of a slab.

Attics and Roofs

As with the encapsulated crawl space, we do not want to bring hot, humid air into an attic. Other than the obvious reason of reducing opportunities for mold and mildew, there are several other advantages. The HVAC components in an attic are in conditioned space and will have less heat gain in the summer. Less heat gain equals less stress, which means the system will last longer. The attic will also be a much more comfortable environment to perform equipment maintenance and a more secure place to store possessions, since they won't be exposed to mold and mildew.

For the water control layer, we use a peel-and-stick roofing underlayment, which has the additional advantage of being considered a secondary roof. (Many home insurance companies offer a policy discount if this product is used.) The air barrier and the thermal barrier will be at the roof, either below or above the roof deck, depending on its detailing. Air-conditioning is the most important aspect of the encapsulated, or enclosed, attic.

Early in our career, we learned the importance of incorporating the most current building science. The case study that follows chronicles some of the issues we encountered that first caused us to question the building codes of the time. In the next chapter, we will take a look at how building science helps us build beautiful, sustainable, healthy homes by examining the nature of the materials used in home design.

All postrenovation photographs in this case study courtesy of Dickson Dunlap

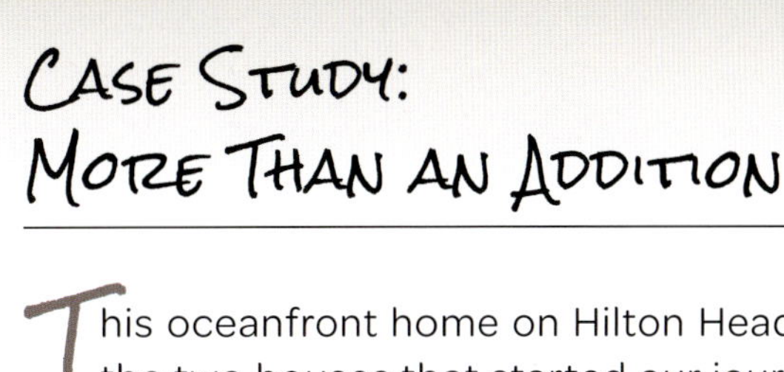

Case Study: More Than an Addition

This oceanfront home on Hilton Head Island is one of the two houses that started our journey into building science and sustainability. What started as an addition and window replacement project turned into a major home reinvention. We peeled back the layers to realize what the home needed, and this discovery inspired us to honor the space with the materials to make it look as it should have from day one.

The home was built in the early '80s as a spec house. After the builder went bankrupt, the house sat unfinished until it was finally completed by another builder. The building materials appeared to have been selected from the reject pile at the building supply store; the quality of the construction was marginal at best (for example, casement windows were installed horizontally instead of vertically).

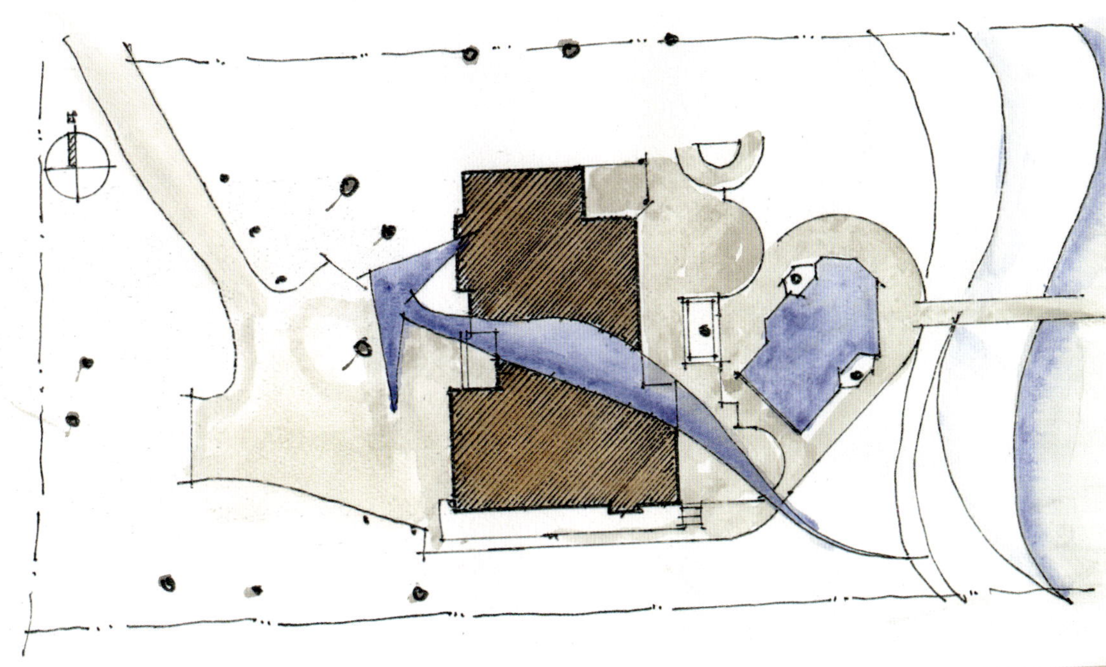

Initially, the renovation involved replacing the windows, siding, and the roof and adding a small addition to the second floor. The clients liked the layout and the feel of the house . . . just not the details. However, after removing the home's exterior skin, we discovered substandard framing, rot, mold, and mildew. So we decided to gut the entire house and took this opportunity to redesign all the interior cabinetry and the stairs, bathrooms, lighting, fireplace, doors, hardware, and floors. We also reworked the exterior paving and decks. We added an outdoor fireplace and grill area. We kept the existing swimming pool. We added many more windows in the kitchen to take advantage of the ocean view.

ABOVE: Front of the house before the renovation

RIGHT: Rear of the house before the renovation

The spaces in the house had a contemporary feel, but all the existing finishes were very traditional. The hodgepodge nature of the finishes also did not allow the house to flow. We selected new finishes in a warm palette, bird's-eye maple with a cherry accent for the cabinets, cherry flooring, maple doors, and limestone in the master bathroom. The exterior shingles were stained a warm gray. The cabinets have clean lines with a cutout corner for the pull, with a cherry backstop behind the cutout. The stair rail is a custom made of steel and wood.

The house now has clean contemporary interiors suitable for the lines of the house and its spectacular oceanfront site.

More Than an Addition: Sustainable Strategies

VERNACULAR

- Renovating an existing house is more sustainable than building new
- House was already oriented to the prevailing breezes

CONTEMPORARY

- Impact-clad casement windows with SHGC less than 0.25
- Drainage plane
- Hurricane upgrades from the existing house
- High-efficiency 18 SEER heat pump with ERV
- VOC-free paint
- All electric
- Conditioned attic and crawl spaces

Project Completed: 2003

Builder: Bay 10 Construction
Hilton Head Island, South Carolina

CHAPTER 5
Materials for Health, Durability & Aesthetics

"Until the last blink of human civilization all buildings were fashioned from materials at hand and only minimally processed from their natural state . . . With the proliferation of mass-produced petrochemical-based products and chemicals for construction that began post-WWII . . . we have released a Pandora's box of toxins into our home."

—Paula Baker-Laporte, FAIA, and John Banta, CIH, *Prescriptions for a Healthy House*

Over our forty-year careers, the criteria for selecting building materials have evolved dramatically. Early in our careers, materials were selected on the basis of aesthetics, availability, durability, and cost. In the early years of the 2000s, when certification programs such as LEED for Homes were developed, environmental impacts were added to the criteria. Materials that factor in these impacts included wood certified by the Forest Stewardship Council (FSC), salvaged materials, products with recycled content, local materials, and low or no emissions of volatile organic compounds (VOCs). Best practices today build on all the above and consider the impact of the life cycle of the material. To select materials wisely, we have to understand what is in them, how they were made, and if they can be recycled at the end of their usefulness.

Material selection impacts our health, the health of our communities, and the health of our planet. Our choice of materials can have an impact on our health both positively though biophilia design and negatively if there are toxic ingredients in the product. In addition, how materials are extracted or manufactured can have a negative effect on our communities through environmental pollutants. The embodied carbon from extracting materials, manufacturing them, and transporting them to their building site is a leading cause of global warming. The less carbon that gets released into the world, the better off our planet will be. Selecting environmentally responsible building products is critical to reducing the carbon footprint and creating healthy buildings.

Courtesy of Kim Smith

Considering that we spend on average 87 percent of our time in buildings and 68 percent of that in our homes (according to the EPA), it is essential that we select the best materials for our projects. This is often easier said than done when weighing the pros and cons of particular products. A product might be very durable, such as cementitious siding, but have a high level of embodied carbon. Or it might be both inexpensive and durable, such as luxury vinyl tile, but is a petrochemical product that off-gases chemicals, and its manufacture spews pollutants into the atmosphere.

Corey Squire provides an intuitive and easy explanation of how to best consider the building materials for your home design:

> Choosing materials or products that are simple, natural, and local will generally result in better outcomes. Simple means containing fewer ingredients or chemical components. . . . Natural means minimally processed and closest to the form in which it was extracted . . . and finally, choosing locally extracted and manufactured products that have shorter and simpler supply lines can provide quality assurance for equitable labor practices and reporting accuracy.

In this chapter, we will examine how the materials we select affect global warming by determining the embodied carbon of those materials. Some products have an inherently higher embodied-carbon footprint than others. We will explore ways to lower the embodied carbon footprint of your home and also look at material sourcing from many aspects, including the use of local, salvaged, recycled, and sustainable materials. We will also dive into how to select safe, nontoxic materials. The goal is to create a beautiful, healthy home built of durable, environmentally friendly, nontoxic materials that will last for generations.

About twenty years ago, architect Edward Mazria, FAIA founder of Architecture 2030, wrote an article called "Architects Pollute!" for *Metropolis* magazine. Mazria suggested that the environmental impact of climate change fell directly on the architectural profession. The built environment contributes over 42 percent of the annual global CO_2 emissions; 27.3 percent is from building operations, and 15 percent is from the embodied carbon of just four materials: iron, steel, aluminum, and the portland cement in concrete. We can reduce CO_2 emissions from the building operations through tight building enclosures and efficient building systems (which we cover in the next chapter).

We all have a really important role to play in carbon reduction through sustainable design and the selection of materials. The following strategies can help reduce the embodied carbon in our buildings. Renovating a building instead of building a new one is often an excellent option, because the carbon has already been spent to build the existing building. Likewise, using salvaged materials and material with high postconsumer recycled content saves on carbon emission.

Design for an Efficient Use of Resources

According to the EPA, an average-size home (2,400 square feet) generates 8,000 pounds of construction waste, with 40 to 50 percent of it being wood. Designing with material sizes in mind reduces that waste; overall dimensions on a 2-foot module is the most efficient for stud spacing, drywall, and sheet materials. Often, traditional framing methods can use 15 to 20 percent more material than is structurally needed. Advanced framing uses techniques to reduce the amount of lumber and waste in the building. It saves money both in construction costs and in operations because with less lumber, there is more space for insulation. The EPA reports that using advanced framing can save up to 5 percent on annual heating and cooling costs and between 3 and 5 percent in labor cost. When considering advanced framing, first check with your structural engineer to ensure that the design meets all of the wind, seismic, and other design loads for your location.

ADVANCED FRAMING

- 2 × 6 wood wall studs 24 inches OC (on center)
- Floor joist and roof rafters 24 inches OC aligned over wall studs
- Two-stud corner framing
- Eliminate window and door headers in non-load-bearing walls
- Single top plates instead of double top plates
- Header hangers instead of jack studs

Carbon-Sequestering Materials

These materials play a crucial role in reducing greenhouse gas concentrations and promoting environmental sustainability. They absorb and store carbon dioxide from the atmosphere, mitigating climate change. Examples include certain building materials such as sustainably sourced wood, hemp, cork, and Venetian plaster, which we've used in our office as well as in a few of our projects.

All new wood used in a house should be FSC certified and have a FSC chain-of-custody (COC) certificate. This standard guarantees sustainable, responsible forest management, promoting environmental conservation, community engagement, and responsible wood production practices.

Venetian plaster is an ancient material that also cleans the air. It's composed of slaked lime and marble dust. The plaster not only creates a luxurious finish but also exhibits carbon-sequestering benefits. As it cures, the plaster reabsorbs carbon dioxide from the air, contributing to a reduced carbon footprint and enhanced environmental sustainability. In one of our projects, when the client didn't like the existing tile on the fireplace, we had the idea to use Venetian plaster to cover it; the result was beautiful. We saved carbon by not demolishing the tile, which also kept it out of the landfill. Instead, we added a layer of material that constantly improves the air quality of the home.

Venetian plaster is a natural material made from lime and does not emit any volatile organic compounds (VOCs).

Reclaimed Materials and Recycled Content

Using reclaimed materials and materials with high recycled content in construction helps our climate by decreasing the demand for virgin resources. The US Green Building Council defines recycled content as "a material that includes at least 25 percent postconsumer or 50 percent preconsumer (postindustrial) recycled material."

Recycling in this way reduces energy-intensive extraction and manufacturing, resulting in lower greenhouse gas emissions. By diverting materials from landfills and incineration, recycling conserves resources and minimizes pollution. It also diminishes environmental degradation associated with resource extraction.

We like to use river-recovered cypress and heart pine because the patina is so beautiful. About 150 years ago, people would float logs down the local rivers to the mills, and many sank in the process. Now people dive for and recover these "sinker logs," which have been preserved in the cool water.

All the walls and cabinets are made from river-recovered cypress. *Courtesy of John McManus*

Choose Materials That Are Manufactured Responsibly

Materials that are extracted, manufactured, and transported with renewable energy will have a smaller carbon footprint than those using fossil fuels. Also, materials that were extracted and manufactured close to the construction site have a smaller carbon footprint because transportation is minimized. It is important to understand the supply chain, because a product may be manufactured locally but the material within it could be from far away.

Lowcountry style, but with a unique twist, is an idea we have gotten pretty familiar with. We believe that houses should be integrated into their place—they should belong. One way to achieve this goal is to use building materials that are native or made here in the Lowcountry. The house often features tabby (a concrete aggregate made with oystershell), handmade brick, and native wood species.

Limit High-Embodied-Carbon Products

Portland cement (used in concrete) and steel are among the highest embodied-carbon materials used in construction today. But many technological advances have begun to lower the carbon footprint of these high-carbon materials.

Even though steel is composed of 93 percent recycled material and is 100 percent recyclable, according to the American Institute of Steel Construction (AISC), its production still emits the highest amount of carbon into the atmosphere, per the EPA. The good news the EPA reports is that American steel companies have reduced their emissions by 30 percent since the 1990s and are committed to lowering them more. Most of the world's steel is produced in China, where the greenhouse gas emissions are three times higher than equivalent products produced in the US, according to the AISC. The use of steel should be limited in home construction, using FSC-certified wood instead. When structural steel is required due to wind or seismic loads, make sure it is manufactured in the United States.

A tabby and brick fireplace. *Courtesy of Kim Smith*

Steel production emits the highest amount of carbon into the atmosphere, and the production of portland cement is a close second, according to the EPA. Since the foundation constitutes most of the concrete used in single-family homes, one way to lessen the amount of concrete used is to change the foundation to wood piles.

The National Ready Mixed Concrete Association (NRMCA) offers several alternatives to reducing the amount of portland cement in a concrete recipe. The most common is to add a supplementary cementitious material such as fly ash, slag cement, or silica fume, which are the most common additives. Other options include volcanic ash, rice husk ash, and ground glass pozzolan. The NRMCA reports that replacing 50 percent of the portland cement with a 50 percent fly ash / slag mixture can reduce the carbon footprint by 40 percent. This type of mixture has been called "green concrete." These substitutes not only help reduce the consumption of natural resources but also mitigate the emission of greenhouse gases associated with cement production. Green concrete represents a significant advancement toward achieving more sustainable infrastructure and building solutions.

Another sustainable option is to sequester carbon dioxide in concrete. According to the NRMCA, this can be accomplished by using demolished crushed concrete as the aggregate in new concrete. They recommend that the demolished crushed concrete should be exposed to the air, where it can absorb carbon dioxide, for one to two years.

Is Your House Making You Sick?

A client hired us to design a Living Building-certified home, which is one of the most rigorous certification programs for sustainable, healthy buildings. He was living in a waterfront house in Charleston, South Carolina, that he built about twenty years ago. The wow feature in the existing house was a waterfall in the dining room. The new house was put on hold because he became extremely ill, and he could not determine what was making him sick. It turned out that the cool waterfall feature created a huge toxic mold problem, from which it took him years to recover.

We've all heard stories about people who've gotten sick from their homes. How and why is this so common? During the 1970s energy crisis, when building enclosures became much tighter, people began to suffer from "sick building syndrome." Without enough fresh air entering the building, carbon dioxide and VOCs build up and can cause serious health issues. When homes were first sealed up tighter, they didn't have the proper air circulation required to keep the air healthy to breathe, and toxic materials that had been used in the construction of homes began to make residents sick. The best defense against the potential risk of unhealthy chemicals infiltrating your home is to circulate the air in the house often. When the air is circulated, it flushes out any pollutants in the air.

Toxic materials can off-gas, causing chemicals to evaporate and disperse into the air. Off-gassing is just one example of how chemicals can get into our environment. Leaching, degradation, and oxidation are also ways that we can unknowingly be exposed to dangerous chemicals in our home. The "sick building syndrome" epidemic finally caused regulators to address the problems caused by exposure. We will look at some watershed events on the road to healthy home design.

Toxic Substances Control Act

The Toxic Substances Control Act (TSCA), a US federal law regulating the manufacture, use, and distribution of chemicals, was enacted in 1976. At the time that the TSCA was instituted, it grandfathered over 62,000 chemicals. Even with the 2016 update to the law, the majority of chemicals have never been tested. Today there are over 80,000 chemicals registered in the United States.

> The true burden of environmentally induced cancer has been grossly underestimated. With nearly 80,000 chemicals on the market in the United States—many of which are used by millions of Americans in their daily lives and are unstudied or understudied and largely unregulated—exposure to potential environmental carcinogens is widespread. (President's Cancer Panel 2010)

There are complex reasons why the United States has not banned the toxic materials that have been banned in other countries. Some have to do with well-funded manufacturers' lobbies, while other involve the lengthy process that it takes to get toxic materials banned in the US. When a material is identified as harmful, it is usually placed under a voluntary ban. And when the United States has banned a product, it is often replaced with one that hasn't been properly tested to make sure that it isn't also harmful to the health of occupants. Europe and other countries are quicker to get the toxins off the market.

A great example is how lead-based paint was banned in Europe about seventy years before it was banned in the US. The world knew that it was bad before the US finally had the political will to ban lead paint. In fact, as early as 1786, Benjamin Franklin wrote a letter to a friend of his, physician Benjamin Vaughn, about the lead poisoning he experienced as an apprentice typesetter in London. The following is an excerpt from that letter.

> In 1724, being in London, I went to work in the Printing-House of Mr. Palmer, Bartholomew Close, as a Compositor. I then found a Practice I had never seen before, of drying a Case of Types, (which are wet in Distribution) by placing it sloping before the Fire . . . But an old Workman observing it, advis'd me not to do so . . . This, with a kind of obscure Pain that I had sometimes felt as it were in the Bones of my Hand when working over the Types made very hot, induc'd me to omit the Practice. ("Benjamin Franklin Experienced Symptoms of Lead Poisoning from Typesetting During His Apprenticeship," historyofinformation.com)

He went on in the letter to cite examples of people in Europe who had contracted digestive problems when drinking rainwater that had been drained into cisterns from leaded roofs and other maladies. Franklin spent the rest of his life telling the public about the toxic nature of lead.

About one hundred years later, in 1886, Germany was the first European country to protect its citizens from lead. They banned women and children from working in factories that manufactured lead-based paints. France followed and banned the use of lead in all buildings in 1909.

Almost seventy years later, the Consumer Product Safety Commission (CPSC) in the United States banned the sale of lead-based paint for residential use in 1978 (the ban of lead-based paint for commercial use began in 1971). The ban was part of the Federal Hazardous Substances Act (FHSA), and it applied to paints containing more than 0.06 percent lead by weight. This regulatory action aimed to address the well-documented health hazards associated with lead exposure, particularly in children, and it marked a significant step toward reducing lead-related health risks in the US.

Because we know so little about the toxicity of chemicals registered in the United States, many environmental scientists promote the precautionary principle, which flips the equation to avoiding untested chemicals instead of using them until they are proven safe or unsafe. The precautionary principle has been adopted by many architects, including us, to help us in the complex journey of specifying safe, nontoxic materials.

How to Spot Toxic Building Ingredients

Like Corey said earlier in this chapter, when you build with natural materials, it's easy to know that they are safe. However, when we begin to look at the wide variety of manufactured materials that could be potentially used, it's important to be familiar with the red flags that indicate harmful chemicals. Here are the most important red flags to watch out for when sourcing materials for your home.

VOCs (Volatile Organic Compounds)—Wet-Applied Products (Paints, Glues, and Sealants)

This group of carbon-based chemicals easily evaporates into the air. They are emitted from wet-applied products such as paints, glues, and sealants. Make sure that the glues in wood products are urea-free formaldehyde. Indoors, VOCs can contribute to poor air quality, leading to health issues. Exposure to VOCs is associated with respiratory problems, headaches, and long-term health risks. Reducing VOC emissions involves using low-VOC or VOC-free products, ensuring proper ventilation, and choosing materials that meet stringent emission standards for healthier indoor environments and decreased environmental impact.

Phthalates—Flexible Vinyl

These synthetic chemicals are commonly used as plasticizers to enhance flexibility and durability in various consumer products, including vinyl flooring, carpet backing, vinyl wall coverings, and flexible ductwork. They can leach into the air, water, and soil and have both carcinogenic and hormone-disrupting potential. Phthalate-free alternatives such as bio-based plasticizers—soy-based plasticizers, for example—reduce environmental and health impacts associated with these chemical compounds.

Flame Retardants

Flame retardants can be found in fabric and upholstery and also on carpets, on carpet backing, and in flame-resistant paints; though intended to enhance fire resistance, they often pose health and environmental risks. Common flame retardants, such as polybrominated diphenyl ethers (PBDEs) and chlorinated organophosphates, can migrate from textiles and accumulate in the environment. Studies link these chemicals to adverse health effects, including developmental issues and hormonal disruptions. Additionally, flame retardants can also break down into toxic byproducts. Concerns about their persistence and potential harm have led to regulatory scrutiny and a shift toward alternative, less toxic flame-retardant formulations. Flame-retardant fabrics are required by code in commercial and public buildings such as schools, hotels, and hospitals but not in single-family residences.

Antimicrobials and Stain Resistance

Perfluorooctanoic acid compounds (PFAs) and biocides pose significant environmental and health hazards. PFAs, used in antimicrobials and stain avoidance, are persistent in the environment and are linked to health issues, including reproductive problems. Biocides, employed as antimicrobial agents in textiles and consumer goods, can contribute to antibiotic resistance. Both PFAs and biocides are strictly regulated because they can accumulate in wildlife and humans, with potential long-term effects on human health and the broader environment.

Asbestos, Lead, Mercury, and Polychlorinated Biphenyls

These are all banned or highly regulated materials that might be present in older, existing buildings. If you encounter any of these materials in a renovation project, seek licensed hazardous removal experts for the demolition.

Identifying Safe Materials

With so many materials available and many of them potentially harmful to your health, where do homeowners turn to get the help they need to make informed choices? Fortunately, many independent organizations have completed the vetting of thousands of products. They include the following:

- Architecture 2030—Mindful Materials (https://www.mindfulmaterials.com/)
- International Living Future Institute—Declare database (https://living-future.org/declare/)
- BuildingGreen—Product Insights (https://www.buildinggreen.com/product-guidance)
- Origin Build (https://origin.build/#/)
- Spot UL (https://spot.ul.com/)
- EC3 (https://www.buildingtransparency.org/)

If the product you want to use is not covered by any of the organizations listed above, the next step is to ask the manufacturer for the Health Product Declaration (HPD). The HPD Collaborative (https://www.hpd-collaborative.org/hpdc-welcome/) developed the HPD as a voluntary reporting standard for manufacturers to report the chemicals in their products. Fortunately, many manufacturers are participating.

However, this is an optional activity, so they may or may not be available for your use. If they are, look at the chemicals listed and check it with the Perkins &

Wills Precautionary List (https://transparency.perkinswill.com/lists/precautionary-list) or the ILFI's Red List (https://living-future.org/red-list/) to determine whether you want to use a product or not.

Both of these lists are free online resources that identify harmful chemicals found in building materials. The lists serve as a transparency tool, helping designers avoid substances detrimental to human and environmental health. The goal is to encourage the use of safer alternatives in construction projects.

Circular Economy

> "If we think about things having multiple lives, cradle to cradle, we could design things that can go back to either nature or back to industry forever."
> —William McDonough, coauthor of *Cradle to Cradle: Remaking the Way We Make Things*

It's important to consider the life cycle of the materials we source in our homes. The environmental impact of all the phases of a building's life cycle must be considered—procurement, construction, operations, and decommissioning. A circular economy is an economic system designed to minimize waste and maximize resource efficiency. It aims to redefine traditional take-make-dispose production models by prioritizing the continual use, recycling, and regeneration of materials. In a circular economy, products are designed for longevity, repairability, and recyclability, and waste is minimized through such practices as reusing, refurbishing, and recycling. The goal is to create a sustainable, closed-loop system that reduces environmental impact, conserves resources, and fosters economic resilience.

To encourage a circular economy, William McDonough and Michael Braungart developed Cradle to Cradle (C2C), an innovative design framework that envisions products and materials as part of a regenerative cycle, promoting sustainability and environmental responsibility. C2C encourages the creation of products designed for infinite reuse or recycling, emphasizing safe materials, renewable energy, and social responsibility. Assessing products on the basis of five quality categories—material health, clean air and climate protection, water and soil stewardship, social fairness, and product circularity—C2C strives for positive impacts on ecosystems and human health. For example, the C2C certifies several kinds of green, sustainable carpet tiles. When it's time to get rid of them, you send them back to the manufacturer, who grinds them up and uses them to make new carpets. This way, the product never goes into the landfill.

A tool to determine the life cycle environmental impact of a product is the manufacturer's Environmental Product Declaration (EPD). This is also a voluntary report that includes information on the environmental impact of raw material acquisition; energy use and efficiency; emissions to air, soil, and water; and waste generation. They also include global warming impact and the life cycle assessment.

How to Choose Materials

We have had clients who became paralyzed when confronting the selection of materials by focusing on the idea that there is the one perfect material for the project. We had one client who would say, "I love this tile, but is there another tile in the entire world that I would love more?" We have found that focusing on some core principles helps narrow the selection process. The concept that was developed for the overall design will also help in material selection.

Is the Material Suitable for a Hot, Humid Climate?

A great example is houses made from straw bales. They are more energy efficient, less expensive, and toxin free, and they sequester carbon and promote healthier indoor air quality. Sounds like the perfect material—except these houses should not get wet and are vulnerable to persistent high humidity, so they are not appropriate for hot, humid climates.

Is the Material Durable?

Most of our projects have aluminum roofs, because they are extremely durable and last three to four times as long as asphalt shingles. Solar panels are easily mounted on them. Leaves and debris slide right off,

This client has always loved this banana leaf wallpaper, so once the decision was made to use the wallpaper, every other selection was easy. *Courtesy of Kim Smith*

and with cool-roof coatings, they reflect the sun's heat. Aluminum roofs are also recyclable at the end of their life. Durable materials typically require less maintenance, which is often a high priority for our clients.

Is the Material Safe?

Is it safe for the occupants, the community, and the workers? Use the precautionary principle in selecting the materials. A current example of a material that is safe once it is installed in your home but is not safe for the workers installing it is engineered stone (quartz). It was recently banned in Australia due to a years-long campaign by doctors, trade unions, and workers because of the cases of silicosis among those involved in its cutting and fabrication. With this new development, we are no longer specifying quartz.

Does the Material Add to the Joy of Your Daily Life?

Does the material function well in its application and is it beautiful? Our projects have large roof overhangs, as we mentioned in the last chapter. Since the roof is not insulated in the overhang, we expose the rafter tails and add cypress sheathing. With a cypress interior ceiling, it is beautiful to look out the window and see the flow of the cypress from inside to outside.

Does It Have a Low Carbon Footprint?

Quite often you will have to consider all of the principles above in making this decision. Going back to the aluminum roof example, it has a higher carbon footprint in manufacturing, but in comparison to asphalt shingles it lasts three times longer. Aluminum is recycled at the end of its use, while asphalt shingles will be replaced three times over the life of the metal roof and are typically not recycled, so they will be added to the landfill. And asphalt doesn't perform as well as metal roofs in a hot, humid climate. A beautiful, durable material will last longer, and you will be less likely to replace it after fifteen years when another material might be either dated or worn out. Thus, the ultimate carbon footprint of the aluminum roof will be lower than that of asphalt shingles.

When selecting materials for a home, we are inspired by Corey Squire and try to use simple, natural, and local materials. We love the beauty of materials that belong to a place. One example is the view looking out over hill towns in Italy, where the roofs blend into the countryside because they are all made from the same local clay. The palette looks exactly as it should because local materials contribute to the sense of place. When you use local materials, they just feel like they belong. And this gives those materials a unique aesthetic quality. The backdrop of your life becomes the palette that's reflective of your natural surroundings.

A cypress ceiling and sheathing with exposed rafter tails

Courtesy of Kim Smith

CASE STUDY: QUONSET HUT RENOVATION

This is the ultimate recycling project. We turned a 1940s Quonset hut into an award-winning home and limited the number of materials with a concrete floor and a stucco exterior. The cabinets are metal and ultimately recyclable at the end of their life.

Reusing and reworking an existing structure is typically less expensive than starting from scratch and infinitely more sustainable. When you move into an existing house, you make the house work for you as best you can. But if you're building a custom home or doing a major renovation, you get to think about how you live and design the house around your life.

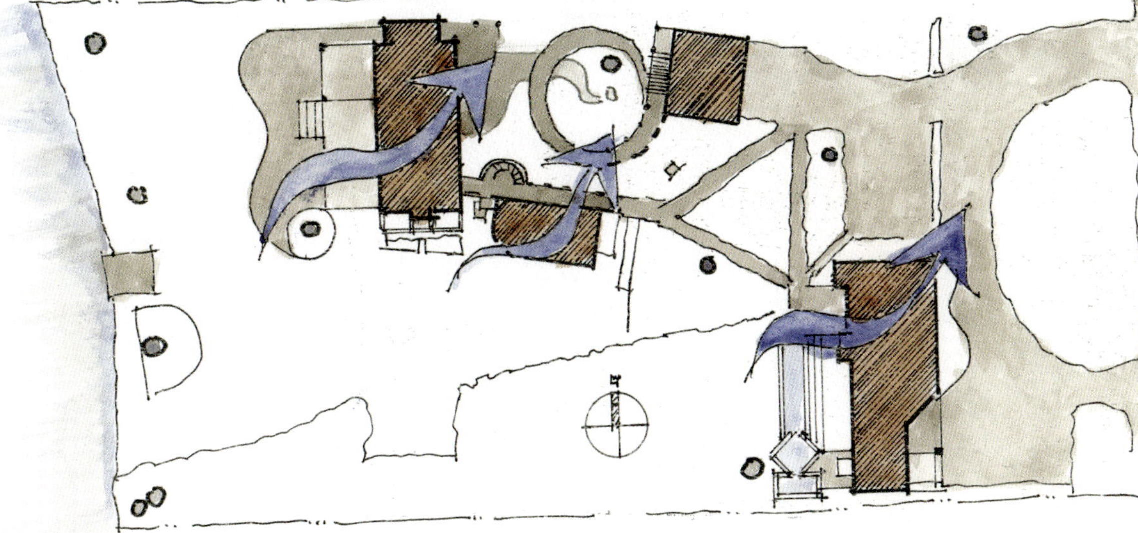

In the beginning of the renovation, we had a complicated job of figuring out how to sensitively attach an addition to the Quonset hut. The hut originally had two bedrooms, two baths, a living room, and a kitchen. There was a funky addition that blocked the views to the river. We removed the addition and opened the Quonset hut to include the living room, dining room, and kitchen.

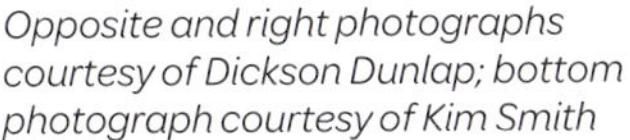

Opposite and right photographs courtesy of Dickson Dunlap; bottom photograph courtesy of Kim Smith

On the end of the hut, we attached a small laundry room and then built a screened-in hallway with a spiral staircase that led to our bedroom on the first floor. By using exterior spaces as our halls, we reduced the amount of conditioned space, which has saved us energy and expense. Upstairs, we created two bedrooms for our girls with a jack-and-jill bathroom. Later, we converted those rooms into a single bedroom with a sitting area and a small kitchenette as a mother-in-law suite.

Courtesy of Dickson Dunlap

Courtesy of Kim Smith

We began the remodel by tearing out everything and took the hut down to its metal shell, leaving the original foundation. Renovation saves a lot of carbon because the carbon has already been spent. The concrete slab is the finished floor. The decision to limit the finish layer lowered the embodied carbon, because otherwise the additional finish layer would have had to be manufactured, delivered, and applied.

We added to the structure to tie down the hut and ensure its resilience in the event of a hurricane.

Courtesy of Kim Smith

It's fun to get creative and resourceful when recycling materials. When we did our renovation in 1992, the movie *Forrest Gump* was being filmed in Beaufort. A contractor whom we knew built and then demolished the movie set of Forrest's childhood home. All the floors in our guesthouse and the interior doors were salvaged from the movie set and saved from the landfill. Sometimes materials just find you if you keep your eyes open.

Courtesy of Dickson Dunlap

Courtesy of Kim Smith

Our house has been our laboratory, and, as we have learned more about sustainability, we've made changes. One significant, sustainable change involved creating a conditioned attic instead of a vented one. This helped keep moisture out of the house and prevented us from incurring the mold damage we'd seen in other houses at the start of our building science journey. We also replaced our old 5-gallon toilets with dual-flush WaterSense models and incorporated WaterSense low-flow faucets. Our heat pumps have also been upgraded over the years to high SEER (Seasonal Energy Efficiency Ratio) units, making them more energy efficient, and that has saved us money on utility bills. Adding a clothesline has also been a sweet way for us to connect with the land and reduce our carbon footprint. As we continue on the Quonset hut's sustainable, resilient journey, we plan to replace our windows with highly efficient impact windows, add solar panels with a battery backup, and replace the gas range with an induction model.

Sustainable landscaping and outdoor living are passions of ours. During various home renovations over the years, we've added different types of exterior living spaces, including a terrace, where we love to entertain. When we bought the house, the 1-acre yard was covered in scraggly grass. In the years since then, we've reduced the amount of grass and planted over forty trees in the yard, adding habitat for the wildlife we enjoy. Our driveway is made of pine straw, which is pervious.

Courtesy of Kim Smith

As we've worked with dozens of homeowners on custom homes and major renovations, we've noticed that one of their biggest misconceptions is the idea that building or renovating a sustainable, resilient home for a hot, humid climate will be expensive. In reality, many of the costs of the design and materials have quick returns on investment. But for those of us with demanding budgets, these changes can be introduced in phases over a period of time, like we have accomplished at our Quonset hut. As the building and science research develops, new sustainable and resilient discoveries can always be phased in as desired.

Courtesy of Kim Smith

Quonset Hut Renovation: Sustainable Strategies

VERNACULAR

- Reused existing structure
- Exterior circulation
- Exterior living

CONTEMPORARY

- Conditioned attic
- Blower door tests
- VOC-free paint
- High-efficiency HVAC unit
- LED lights
- Reclaimed floor in guesthouse
- Reclaimed interior doors
- Concrete floor to minimize finishes
- Energy Star refrigerator, dishwasher, and washing machine
- Clothesline
- WaterSense plumbing fixtures and faucets
- Sheet-metal kitchen cabinets
- Office on the property
- Added trees
- Pervious driveway

Project Completed: Originally built in 1946, first renovation in 1992, second renovation in 2007, additional small interventions in 2012, 2014, and 2021

Builder: Powell Brothers
Beaufort, South Carolina

Courtesy of John McManus

CHAPTER 6
Systems

"A house is a machine for living in."

—Le Corbusier

In our vernacular precedents, there was only one system: a fireplace for heat. Everything else was by design—from the way the house was oriented on its site to the form of the building. As central heating, electricity, plumbing, and air-conditioning were invented and became available, they were added piecemeal to the building design. Today, with tight building enclosures and sustainability at the forefront of design, we must look at all these systems as an integrated whole. By doing so, the home essentially becomes "a machine for living in."

In this chapter, we will cover the different critical systems of the home—mechanical, electrical, and plumbing—and discuss their various sustainability components and how they are integrated into the whole.

Heating, Ventilation, and Air-Conditioning (HVAC)

> A correctly sized cooling system runs long enough to "wring" moisture out of the air. This allows you to be comfortable at a slightly higher thermostat setting and allows you to save money on your utility bill. It also takes care of the "mugginess" without making you feel too cold ("Buyers Beware: Correctly Sized Air Conditioners Save Money!," ashrae.org).

The HVAC home design is often based on rules of thumb tied to the square footage of a house, which produces a poorly performing system. In houses with a very tight building enclosure, this can result in oversized HVAC units that cannot properly remove the humidity. We have yet to find a local mechanical engineer who is interested in designing a system for single-family homes—so we design the HVAC in-house. Since we are focusing on hot, humid climates and air-conditioning is part of the system, we are limiting the discussion in this chapter to forced-air systems.

The first step in designing an HVAC system is to calculate the required load—that is, how much cooling and heating is needed to keep the occupants comfortable. The heating load has one component: maintaining the desired temperature. There are two components to air-conditioning: the cooling load and the removal of humidity (called the latent load).

The required load should be calculated using the Air Conditioning Contractors of America (ACCA) Residential Load Calculation Manual, known in the industry as Manual J. The load calculations determine the heating and cooling for each room and take into consideration orientation, the windows and doors, and the building enclosure.

We calculate the load by using energy modeling, which involves computer simulations to predict accurate heating and cooling demands. By allowing for factors such as thermal conductivity and outdoor conditions, our model calculates the required capacity for the HVAC system. An efficient and properly sized system prevents energy waste, promotes cost-effectiveness, and contributes to environmental sustainability.

After determining the required loads, the next step is selecting the equipment. This selection is done in accordance with ACCA's Residential Equipment Selection Manual, known as Manual S. Equipment options include an air conditioner with a separate furnace, boiler, or heat pump.

Heat Pumps

Heat pumps are much better suited than furnaces with a separate air conditioner for the hot and humid climate. Because heat pumps operate as both a heater and an air conditioner, they incorporate a reversible refrigeration cycle to transfer heat either into or out of the home, depending on the desired temperature. Unlike traditional heating methods that generate warmth through combustion, heat pumps do not create energy; they simply transfer it from hot to cold. This process not only ensures year-round climate control but also brings substantial energy savings, which makes it good for our environment.

Heat pumps come as either package systems or split systems. Package systems have one big unit that sits outside the home and creates a large opening in the building enclosure where the duct enters the building and the unit. In comparison, split systems have two components: an indoor unit and an exterior unit.

SPLIT SYSTEMS

Split systems have two types of technologies for the heat source and sink: air source or ground source. Air source heat pumps, when in heating mode, absorb outdoor heat and release it indoors. When the heat pump is in cooling mode, the process is reversed. Air source heat pumps are energy efficient; by harnessing ambient air, they reduce reliance on fossil-fuel-based heating methods, which lowers carbon emissions.

A ground source heat pump (GSHP) harnesses stable ground temperatures for energy-efficient heating and cooling. Recirculating wells are drilled into the earth to circulate a fluid that absorbs or releases heat. When in heating mode, the fluid extracts heat from the ground and transfers that heat indoors. When cooling, the system reverses by expelling indoor heat back into the ground. Despite the higher costs up front, a ground source heat pump offers long-term savings, reduces environmental impact, and performs consistently. They also are quieter. There is a 30 percent federal tax credit on GSHPs (until 2033). Many states also offer tax credits on these units.

CAPACITY

The next differentiator for heat pumps is how much heating or cooling the unit can put out. Most older heat pumps are single stage, meaning they are either on or off. A two-stage heat pump is capable of producing two speeds—low capacity and high capacity—and provides greater efficiency and comfort. The variable-capacity heat pump is the most efficient because it doesn't have set stages; rather, it can vary capacity continuously between the low and high end.

EFFICIENCY

Equipment efficiency should be a major consideration when selecting your system. How can you tell whether your system is efficient? Air source heat pumps and air conditioners rate cooling efficiency by using the seasonal energy efficiency ratio (SEER). The higher the SEER number, the more efficient the unit. In 2023, the minimum required SEER rating for Southern states was 15 SEER. However, the IECC recommends a rating of at least 16 SEER for a more efficient system.

Heating efficiency is measured by the heating season performance factor (HSPF). The required minimum for the Southern states is 8.8 HSPF, with a preferred rating of 10 HSPF.

DUCTS

The next step in the HVAC system design involves sizing and laying out the air ducts and then determining the location of the supply and return grills. A duct's size is based on the ACCA's Manual D, Residential Duct Systems. Ducts should be installed in air-conditioned spaces in a trunk-and-branch system (see "Water Distribution" below) in the straightest, most direct, and shortest route possible. With the exception of the last 15 feet before the register, all ducts should be rigid sheet-metal ducts. The last 15 feet can use flex ducts and should be used only in a straight run. All duct joints should be sealed with mastic sealant and insulated properly.

The air supply and return registers are designed in accordance with ACCA's Manual T, Air Distribution Basic for Residential and Small Commercial Buildings. Design considerations include how well the air circulates (known as "throw"), noise, and comfort.

Installation of a rigid duct with flex ducts to vents

DEHUMIDIFICATION

When addressing humidity, it's important to consider the entire building as a system rather than just the HVAC equipment. An integrated design approach to control humidity must be a priority at the beginning of any home design that incorporates high-performance HVAC equipment combined with proper airflow, ventilation, and construction techniques to create an effective moisture control system.

A correctly sized unit will remove the majority of the moisture from the air. If the HVAC unit is oversized, it may not run long enough to remove the humidity from the air. A separate dehumidifier should be considered if there are regularly large numbers of people in the house or if the building is particularly small, such as guesthouses or rooms over garages.

VENTILATION

Poor ventilation can lead to health issues for homeowners. Without fresh air, a tight building can cause illness such as sick building syndrome (SBS), which can lead to headaches, fatigue, and respiratory issues. Factors such as poor ventilation, mold, and VOCs from household items can also contribute to SBS. The combination of good ventilation, using low-emission materials, and maintaining good indoor air quality is essential for preventing SBS inside the home. Here we will look at both local ventilation and whole-house ventilation.

Local Ventilation

Kitchens, bathrooms, and laundry rooms are the most common spaces for local ventilators. Cooking, especially with gas cooktops, is a significant source of indoor air pollutants. This is why choosing, and using, the right range hood is essential. The capture efficiency is determined by how well the blower captures the particulates generated from cooking. The range hood should be the same size or larger as the cooking surface and should vent to the exterior. A range hood with a remote blower (also called an in-line blower) is much quieter and therefore will be more likely to be utilized than a blower located in the hood itself.

Moving on from the kitchen, bathroom and laundry fans should also be vented to the exterior. These fans can be individual units or part of the whole-house ventilation system with the energy recovery ventilator (ERV), which is discussed in the following section.

Whole-House Ventilation

An energy recovery ventilator (ERV) is a type of ventilation system that is designed to improve air quality indoors while simultaneously optimizing energy

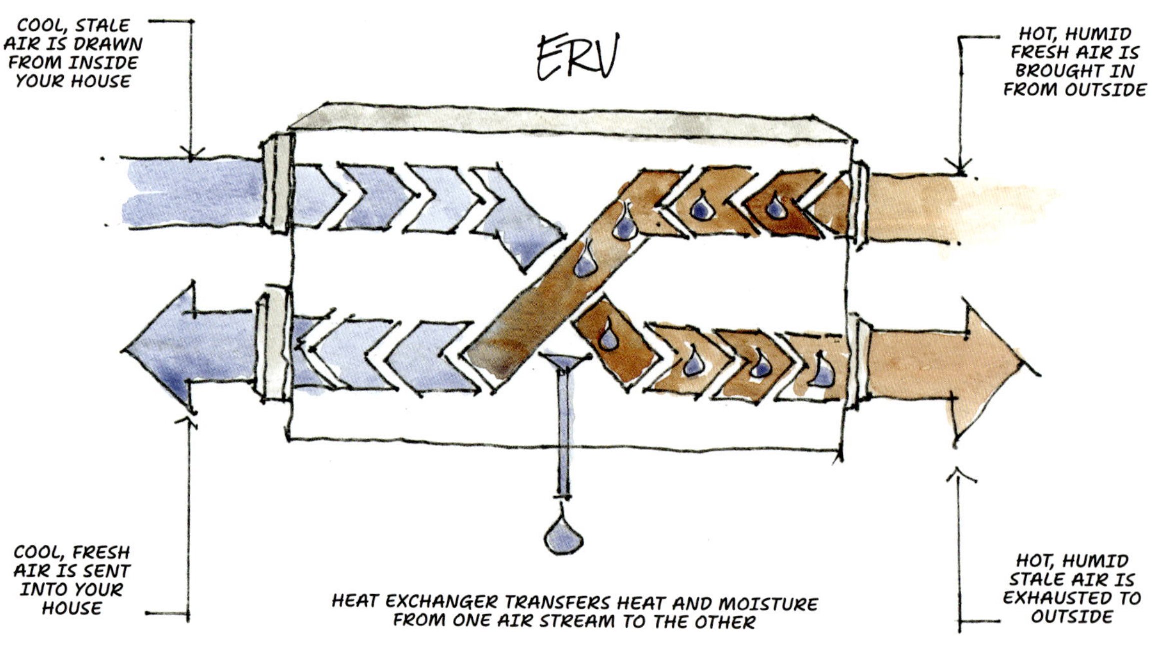

efficiency. The primary function of an ERV is to exchange stale indoor air with fresh outdoor air while also recovering the energy from the outgoing air in the process and removing moisture. ERVs are similar to heat recovery ventilators (HRVs), with the exception that HRVs do not remove moisture from the air.

Plumbing Systems

The plumbing system consists of the heating and distribution of water and the end use at the faucets and fixtures. There are opportunities to save water and energy at each stage of the system, especially considering that heating water is the second-largest use of energy in a home (according to the EPA). In most homes, there is little attention paid to the water distribution system, and this often results in long wait times for hot water, which wastes time, water, and energy.

Hot Water

Heating your water efficiently is critical in getting to net zero. Water heater energy efficiency is determined by the uniform energy factor (UEF). The higher the UEF, the more efficient the unit. However, the UEF should not be the sole factor in selecting a water heater; size, first-hour rating (the number of gallons a water heater can heat per hour), and fuel type should also be considered.

Fuel Type

Water heating options include the type of fuel and whether or not there is a storage tank. The goal for a net-zero home is to be all electric; this is why we recommend using an electric water heater with a storage tank. Tankless electric water heaters, also known as instantaneous water heaters, use a lot of energy, so they should be considered only in unique applications, such as supplying hot water to a sink. With this in mind, the best two options are electric resistance-storage water heaters and electric heat pump storage water heaters. Extremely efficient electric resistance-storage water heaters are around 90 percent efficient. A heat pump water heater is 370 percent efficient and would seem to be the best option, but it does have some drawbacks—it will draw heat out of the surrounding air and is also a bit noisier than an electric resistance-storage water heater.

Water Distribution

Water distribution from the water heater to the end use is often the weak link in the plumbing system—wasting time, water, and energy. The amount of time you must wait for hot water to reach the faucet is the structural waste. This waste is based on the length of pipe between the water heater and faucet, the pipe's diameter and material, and whether the piping is insulated.

A heat pump water heater on the right during installation, with a storage tank on the left

The EPA's WaterSense program has a New Home Specification Guide for Efficient Hot Water Delivery System. Their requirements include the following:

- No more than 0.5 gallons of water may be stored in any piping or manifold between the hot water source and any hot water fixture.
- To account for the additional water that must be removed from the system before hot water can be delivered, no more than 0.6 gallons of water may be delivered to a fixture before the hot water arrives.
- Recirculation systems must be demand-initiated. They may not be solely timer- or temperature-based.

The current guidelines for plumbing pipe sizes are from the 1940s, which results in oversized pipes based on old, high-flow fixtures. The flow rates of faucets and fixtures have been dramatically reduced since the 1992 Energy Policy Act; the supply pipes should be reduced accordingly. Smaller pipes have less structural waste because there is less water in the line. And when using smaller pipes, hot water is delivered more quickly from the water heater.

There are four basic water delivery layout systems: trunk-and-branch, core, whole-house manifold, and demand-initiated recirculation. The common element in designing an efficient water delivery system is laying out the plumbing fixtures as close as possible to the water heater. This includes stacking bathrooms on multiple floors to create proximity.

The trunk-and-branch systems are the most common water delivery layout. The system involves running the main line, with the largest diameter, from the water heater to the farthest fixture, where small-diameter twigs (small pipes) connect to the individual fixtures in between. The trunk-and-branch system is best suited for smaller homes or homes with a limited number of fixtures that can be grouped together.

Core systems employ individual direct lines to each plumbing fixture; this allows all the lines to be much smaller, which in turn reduces waste. Like the trunk-and-branch, the core system is best suited for small homes.

Whole-house manifold systems are often the best option for larger houses. In this system, there is a central manifold located close to the water heater, and small-diameter flexible pipes run to each fixture. There are several advantages to the manifold system. First, flexible piping can be installed faster, and fewer fittings are needed, reducing heat loss as the water moves through the pipe. Manifold systems also equalize pressure, so multiple fixtures can be used at once. This prevents the common problem of drastic variances in water temperature that can occur when someone is showering and someone somewhere else in the house flushes a toilet.

A demand-initiated recirculating system has no structural waste. When the system is activated, a pump recirculates the cool water that has been sitting in the hot water line and returns it to the water heater to be reheated and reused. The system offers more flexibility because it can accommodate longer pipe runs and a less centralized fixture location.

The final pieces of the plumbing system are the faucet and fixtures. It is important that these fixtures are rated WaterSense by the EPA. Often when you're visiting a plumbing supply store, salespeople will push the high-flow faucets (we think it's because they don't want you to come back and complain that there's no water pressure when you shower). But the new low-flow showerheads and faucets are so excellent that you can't even tell they are low flow. They also conserve a valuable resource—water—and save money on electric and water bills too.

Electrical Systems

The final component of getting your home to net zero is the use of electricity. Our journey began by reducing our energy requirements, using the lessons learned from the vernacular precedents. We further decreased our energy use with tight building enclosures and efficient mechanical and plumbing systems.

In this section, we will cover how to reduce energy through the selection of light fixtures and appliances and how to offset the energy you do use with the on-site generation of electricity, using a photovoltaic and battery backup storage system. Light fixtures, appliances, and other electric products in your home should all be Energy Star certified, an independent certification that meets strict energy efficiency standards. According to the EPA, Energy Star and its partners have prevented 4 billion metric tons of greenhouse gas emissions since 1992.

Lighting

Effective lighting design involves thoughtful consideration of layering and designing light fixtures according to each room's various functions. We use ambient lights so you can see while walking through a room, task lights for just those areas where bright light is needed, decorative lights such as chandeliers and wall sconces (as the "jewelry"), and spotlights to draw attention to an object. Strategically layering the lighting in a home combines different types of lighting fixtures to create a functional yet inviting space. The different layers should be on different switches for maximum flexibility.

The natural light in this living room is supplemented with layers of lights from ceiling fixtures and lamps.

Courtesy of John McManus

Consider choosing lighting fixtures that are efficient, beautiful, and Energy Star certified. LED fixtures have emerged as a sustainable and energy-efficient lighting option. LED technology significantly reduces energy consumption, making it an environmentally conscious choice for homeowners.

Color temperature is another critical aspect when it comes to lighting. Maintain a consistent color temperature within a single room to avoid a visually jarring experience. Different activities and spaces benefit from varying color temperatures:

- Warm tones range from 2,500 to 3,000 Kelvin and emulate the cozy glow of traditional incandescent bulbs, suitable for creating a comfortable and inviting atmosphere.
- Neutral tones range from 3,500 to 4,000 Kelvin and are ideal for task-oriented areas, offering clear and focused lighting for workspaces.
- Cooler tones range from 5,000 to 6,000 Kelvin and are suitable for places that demand bright illumination, such as garages.

Use natural light to reduce the amount of energy needed to light a home. Most people consider the windows and skylights when letting natural light into the home; however, we have incorporated solar tubes into our offices and enjoy the light they provide. Solar tubes use mirrors to reflect sunlight into the interior of a room. They are a satisfying alternative to skylights because they provide natural light while avoiding the eyesore of debris and dirt that can build up.

A well-thought-out approach to lighting design encompasses layering, choice of fixture, and color temperature to enhance the practicality, energy efficiency, and ambiance of each room in a home.

Garden Lighting

Most of our houses feature large windows to take advantage of the great landscape views. However, without the proper landscape lighting, those windows become black mirrors at night, which creates a boxed-in feel. Adding a layer of light in the garden connects those inside to the outdoors, even at night, by visually expanding the interior space. Remember, you are not re-creating daylight but enabling a dynamic composition that will enliven the outdoor room.

As with interior lighting, you will want to use different levels of lighting in the garden. For example, task lighting is used for grilling or for reading. These lights are typically downlights and should also be on separate switches from the other exterior lights. Accent lights provide depth and dimension; use these sparingly. Finally, decorative lighting is the finishing touch that welcomes you to the house.

Appliances

Appliance selection is all about making conscious choices. Assess your "needs" versus "wants" to avoid unnecessary duplication (such as multiple refrigerators) and to ensure that each appliance serves a purpose. Invest in Energy Star options to align your appliance needs with practicality, sustainability, and energy conservation.

As mentioned in the previous section, a home's goal is to be net zero, and that means having all electric appliances. Therefore, we recommend installing electric cooktops, ranges, or both. We understand that many people are reluctant to give up their gas stoves, but cooking on a gas stove burns fossil fuels, and standing over a gas stove means that you are breathing in those fumes.

> Gas-burning stoves in kitchens across America may pose a greater risk to the planet and public health than previously thought, new research suggests. The appliances release far more of the potent planet-warming gas methane than the Environmental Protection Agency estimates, Stanford University scientists found in a study published in the journal *Environmental Science and Technology*. The appliances also emit significant amounts of nitrogen dioxide, a pollutant that can trigger asthma and other respiratory conditions. ("Gas Stoves in Kitchens Pose a Risk to Public Health and the Planet, Research Finds," *Washington Post*, January 2022)

Electric induction cooktops are healthier and are gaining in popularity. Many chefs even prefer induction cooktops because the food cooks faster and they can better control the temperature to create a really low simmer. There is also no additional heat that emanates from an electric induction cooktop.

Something else to consider when choosing appliances and other electronics is what is called the vampire, or phantom, load. Essentially, every appliance that has a clock or a light uses power. The power these appliances use when not in use is called the phantom load. Switching outlets or using power strips can help in managing the phantom load.

Photovoltaics

In our hot, humid climate, we cannot reach net zero without on-site power generation. Many clients think that they want a backup generator so that, in the event of a hurricane, they won't lose power. These clients usually opt for solar power once we make the case that, with the addition of a power wall of backup batteries, it's possible to store power for emergency use without

Induction cooktops have a sleek contemporary profile. *Courtesy of Kim Smith*

the need for a generator. After federal and state tax credits, and with net metering, the initial purchase of solar is usually paid back in around six years. (This does not include the added savings from not purchasing a nasty, loud, and fossil-fuel-burning generator.)

We prefer planting or using existing trees to naturally cool our homes, so sometimes solar isn't an option. For example, we have too many trees on our property to install and use solar panels. Our solution was to subscribe to a communal solar farm that sells solar energy to our power company, which is then credited on our electric bill.

Lightning Protection

We recommend lightning protection systems to all of our clients because our region can experience intense thunderstorms. Storm damage can range from loss of electronic equipment to damaged chimneys to total destruction by fire caused by lightning strikes.

"The good news is most personal injury and property damage caused by lightning can be prevented," says Leslie Chapman-Henderson, CEO and president of the Federal Alliance for Safe Homes (FLASH). Bud VanSickle, executive director of the Lightning Protection Institute (LPI), agrees. "Home and business owners needn't take their chances with lightning," Bud explains. "A professionally installed lightning protection system which meets US safety standards . . . will prevent lightning damage by providing a safe electrical path into the earth for lightning's destructive energy."

We recommend having lightning protection installed by someone certified by the LPI to ensure proper installation (you may also receive a discount on your homeowner's insurance). A lightning protection system is composed of rods (also called air terminals), conductors, and ground terminals. The rods do not attract lightning, but if lightning strikes, it will usually strike the rod since it is the tallest part of the building's structure. Conductors channel the electrical current to the ground, and ground terminals dissipate the electrical energy, safeguarding the structure.

While lightning protection systems can be installed at any time, the best time to install them is during new construction, since this makes it easy to hide the cable conductors within the walls. The costs vary depending on the size and complexity of the building. VanSickle estimates that a lightning system will cost about 1 percent of the building's total construction cost. Those costs can be offset with potential savings from home insurance—and the peace of mind that your home is safe from lightning.

Some people overlook the value of this important system. Once we designed a relatively tall house out in the country, and our clients opted not to install lightning protection. Shortly after construction was finished, lightning hit their house. The strike destroyed their chimney and killed all their electronics. Afterward, they decided to have lightning protection installed. However, when you have to retrofit your home with lightning protection, the copper conducting wires are visible on the exterior of the home, compromising its aesthetic appeal.

As you can see, properly installed lightning protection is crucial for homes in the South to minimize potential damage and keep homeowners safe from frequent lightning storms. A certain section of central Florida has the nation's highest number of lightning strikes per year, earning it the name "lightning alley."

To mitigate unwanted damage from spikes in electricity that can arise during storms, install surge protection for your electric systems. Once it is installed on incoming electric lines, if lightning hits a tree in the yard, it won't send a resulting surge through your system and burn up all your electronics.

If you are curious to learn more, we have included in-depth detail on building systems in the book's "Resources and References" section. When you've designed a home with the consideration of all its important systems, you will be better able to be energy efficient and sustainable. Light fixtures and cooktops that don't produce heat mean that you can reduce the size of the air conditioner needed in your home. These changes are small, but the impacts are huge for the homeowner—for their health, their pocketbook, and our planet.

The following case study will walk you through the various systems we've designed in our clients' net-zero home.

All photographs in this case study courtesy of Kim Smith

CASE STUDY: GETTING TO NET ZERO

We designed this home with the intent of enjoying a quiet, intimate moment as the sun sets over the marsh and river and for hosting the whole family on the holidays. It's a wonderful, resilient, and energy-efficient home set on a wooded lot overlooking the Beaufort River, where the owners can enjoy the pleasures of the Lowcountry: sailing, boating, fishing, and golf.

The owners wanted to maximize their view, their connection to the land, and the natural light within the home. A great room is flanked by four 12-foot-wide, 10-foot-tall sliding glass doors. Another sliding glass door connects the kitchen and the screened porch, allowing ample daylight to fill the home.

We designed a calming, neutral interior with the use of a muted color palette. In addition, we brought in natural materials to layer texture and build interest. The fireplace wall is rendered in Venetian plaster, which, when applied in thin layers, creates a soft, earthy look and filters the air.

We designed the house to be extremely energy efficient, with a predicted energy usage that is close to net zero. Our holistic approach to sustainability begins with the placement of the house on the site so that it captures the breezes and utilizes both shade and sun in a thoughtful manner.

The systems incorporated into this design include a superefficient geothermal heat pump that also provides hot water, a 11.9 kW solar panel array and Powerwall batteries, a tight building enclosure, windows with a low solar heat gain coefficient, and occupancy sensors that activate ERVs. The lightning protection system is concealed with the exception of the rods on the roof.

In hurricane-prone Beaufort, resilience is of the utmost importance. This house was raised up one story above the base flood elevation to ensure that its living spaces were above the floodplain. It's structurally designed and built to withstand 140 mph winds and has impact-resistant windows. The large sliding glass doors are further protected by roll-down hurricane screens. In the event of a multiday power outage, the house will remain operational, thanks to the solar panels and backup battery.

Getting to Net Zero: Sustainable Strategies

VERNACULAR

- Placement of the home on the site to take advantage of sun angles and prevailing breezes
- Single-width rooms for cross ventilation
- High ceilings
- Large overhangs
- Raised first floor

CONTEMPORARY

- Net-zero home
- Geothermal heat pumps with an ERV
- Solar panels
- Battery backups
- Energy Star LED lighting
- Venetian plaster
- Low-SHGC glass
- Blower door test
- VOC-free paint
- WaterSense plumbing fixtures
- Heat pump water heater with on-demand recirculating pump activated by motion sensors

Project Completed: 2022

Builder: Broad River Construction & Phifer Construction Services
Beaufort, South Carolina

SECTION III:

Resiliency—FUTURE-PROOFING Design

Courtesy of John McManus

CHAPTER 7
A Port in the Storm

"Resiliency is similar to sustainability, but there is a difference. Sustainability is reducing a building's impact on the environment, and resiliency is reducing the environment's impact on a building or community. Generally, sustainability initiatives add to a building's resiliency, but some resiliency requirements are not as sustainable, especially when they are creating redundancy."

—Jane Frederick, Frederick + Frederick Architects, "The Case for Resiliency"

It's one thing to hear about a hurricane. It's something else entirely to live through one.

In the abstract, you might understand that hurricanes are a threat, but until you face one down, you won't really understand how important it is to be prepared. We still vividly recall our experience while evacuating during Hurricane Hugo in 1989. We had moved to Beaufort in February of that year; Hugo hit in September. The weather forecasts warned that Hugo was rapidly intensifying as it approached the South Carolina coast, so we decided to evacuate to safety at a friend's house in Charlotte, North Carolina. However, in a stroke of bad luck, Charlotte ended up in Hugo's path—and no one there was expecting a hurricane. The eye of the storm passed right over the city, and the resulting devastation was massive due to strong winds and torrential rain. Thousands of huge oak trees fell. We were amazed our car wasn't hit by one of them.

We were the lucky ones. Our friends in McClellanville, South Carolina (just north of Charleston), spent a terrifying night hanging on to the roof rafters as a 20-foot storm surge swelled and overtook the city. Those friends promised never again to stay put—in the future, they will evacuate. Their experience was an early lesson for us in the power of hurricanes and how we need to be prepared for them.

The US Global Change Research Program in the Fifth National Climate Assessment (NCA) reports that since 1980, the Southeast has had a higher frequency of billion-dollar disasters than any other region. The NCA identifies the major climate stressors in the Southeast as extreme heat, extreme precipitation events, drought persistence and strength, sea level change, tornadoes, and hurricanes. Rapid growth throughout the region is exacerbating these threats.

In this chapter, we introduce the four types of resiliencies. Ultimately, the durability and strength of the home can protect against adverse impacts from chronic climate demands, along with unexpected circumstances such as hurricanes, tornadoes, pests, or earthquakes. We will also focus on a few survivability aspects of the home—how home design can allow residents to shelter in place (unless under a mandatory evacuation order), giving them protection during a storm, while also allowing for functional survivability after the storm.

Types of Resiliencies

Architect Lance Hosey identified four kinds of resiliency: climate, functional, community, and aesthetic. Climate resiliency reduces the environmental impact on a building. Depending on the anticipated hazard, buildings and landscapes may be protected or hardened against the elements to withstand natural disasters and rising seas. Other options include adapting or retreating.

We are certified in the Safety Assessment Program (SAP) through the State of California Governor's Office of Emergency Services. We have worked along with other architects and engineers to quickly assess whether damaged buildings are safe enough to inhabit after a disaster. One of the buildings we encountered during our service was on Edisto Beach after Hurricane Matthew (*see image*). As is evident, one of the columns was completely washed out; the house was probably going to collapse soon.

Performing a safety assessment on Edisto Beach, South Carolina, after Hurricane Matthew

Many of the houses we investigated had been built high enough. However, many of the homes had been built in the 1940s and 1950s, before the building codes were adopted. Over the years, homeowners added rooms in the floodplain underneath, and those rooms were wiped out by the storm. The storm surge washed over 3 feet of sand through these homes and into the road on the other side. Waves were still breaking under some of these houses three days after the storm.

Historically, we learn about building performance by experiencing hurricanes such as Andrew in 1992. However, the better, less risky way to learn is through research. The nonprofit Insurance Institute for Business & Home Safety (IBHS) has a research center in Chester County, South Carolina, and performs building testing on full-scale, two-story models in a 21,000-square-foot, six-story-tall building.

The IBHS can create a broad spectrum of weather—ranging from hurricane conditions to windstorms, wildfires, and hailstorms. It uses the data to develop best practices in building construction. The research center also has a "roof farm," an exterior installation to test decay and deterioration caused by severe weather. This allows the center to conduct long-term evaluations of new materials and systems.

We recently had a contractor tell us that impact windows were a waste of money because they can still crack, and the insurance will pay for all the damage anyway. This is false logic. The IBHS research shows that a key mitigation step is protecting the windows and doors with impact-rated products. When the openings of a building are compromised during a hurricane, the pressure imbalances, uplift forces, and dynamic stresses can cause the roof to blow off and the walls to collapse; impact windows will help prevent that from happening, even if they suffer cracks.

ADVANTAGES OF IMPACT WINDOWS AND DOORS

Impact glass is made with two pieces of heat-treated glass laminated together, with a plastic membrane in the middle. The certification process of impact glass windows requires windows to be able to withstand an impact test: A 2 × 4 is fired at the window unit at a rate of 50 feet per second. If the exterior glass shatters, the unit's integrity remains uncompromised due to the plastic membrane in the middle.

Impact windows provide the following:

- Greater noise insulation
- Additional home security
- Reduced insurance cost
- Increased home value
- There is no additional work to do to protect impact windows in advance of a hurricane, as opposed to other types of window protection (such as nailing plywood over windows on the exterior of the home).

Fortunately, South Carolina has stringent building codes. The IBHS rates the United States' eighteen hurricane-prone states based on the quality of their building codes, with a rating of 100 being the highest quality. Of these, South Carolina ranks third, with an IBHS score of 92 (Florida, at 95, and Virginia, at 94, are ranked first and second, respectively).

In 2022, Julie Rochman, the former CEO of IBHS, said, "States with strong, updated codes saw stunning proof this year that updated, well-enforced building codes have led to the construction of homes and buildings that can stand up to fierce hurricane winds. It can't be any clearer: these codes work."

Climate

Climate resiliency is the capacity of a community to anticipate, prepare, respond to, and recover from the adverse impacts of climate change. It focuses on enhancing the ability to withstand and adapt to changing climate conditions, such as extreme weather events, rising sea levels, and temperature fluctuations. There are several components in climate resilience—including health, water, and shelter—as well as a social component that involves the culture or historical traditions needed to maintain a sense of place.

We are ignoring the consequences of building in vulnerable places. Research by the National Institute of Building Sciences (NIBS) found that adopting the latest building codes can save $11 for every $1 invested, while increasing construction cost by only 1 percent (compared to 1990 costs). NIBS also demonstrated that investing in hazard mitigation measures to exceed select building code requirements can save $4 for every dollar.

Functional

Functional resiliency means being able to occupy a building after a disaster strikes. Current building standards and codes focus on preserving lives by reducing the likelihood of significant building damage or structural collapse from hazards. But they generally don't address the additional need to preserve quality of life by keeping buildings habitable so that they can function as normally as possible, what we call "immediate occupancy."

Functional resiliency often incorporates redundant systems. By prioritizing essential functions and designing proactively, it's possible for your home to withstand disruptions from natural disasters and to minimize the impact of adverse events both on the home's design and the homeowner's well-being.

After Hurricane Hugo, there were parts of Charleston that didn't have power for a month, but instead of evacuating, everyone wanted to stay in town to help clean up. If you had a home that had been designed with vernacular principles—and a solar array and battery backup—you could still function in your house. The solar would keep the refrigerator, lights, hot water, and electric range working, and you still could open the windows to capture the prevailing breezes.

Community

Community resiliency is the collective capacity of a community to effectively respond to and recover from challenges such as natural disasters, economic downturns, social crises, and health emergencies. It focuses on municipal and neighborhood resources that help people bounce back to normal.

The National Institute of Standards and Technology's Community Resilience Planning Guide for Buildings and Infrastructure Systems (see "Resiliency," under "Resources and References") provides a practical and flexible approach to help all communities improve their resilience by setting priorities and allocating resources to manage risks for their prevailing hazards. This involves disaster preparedness planning, infrastructure development, and social cohesion initiatives. Resilient communities can better withstand and bounce back from adversity, ensuring the well-being and sustainability of their members while fostering a sense of belonging and mutual support.

Here's a good example: Charleston's mayor Joe Riley set a goal of getting the city's Waterfront Park, under construction when Hugo hit in September, open by its original completion date. The partially built park had been blown away by Hugo, including eighty-six trees and a fountain, causing one million dollars in damage. "I knew it was important to the community—that they knew we succeeded, that we got our park. So, we worked nonstop, and it opened in May—less than a year after the storm. A part of this is community spirit and confidence—we're gonna do this; we made it," Mayor Riley said. Today, Waterfront Park, which includes its iconic pineapple fountain, is a main attraction for people visiting the Lowcountry.

Aesthetic

Aesthetic resilience is best described by the Senegalese environmental engineer Baba Dioum: "In the end, we conserve only what we love." Lance Hosey would always say that sustainable design has to be beautiful, because you're going to protect and keep only what's beautiful. By blending functionality with beauty, promoting creative expression, and respecting local aesthetics, resilient design can enhance the quality of life, promote social well-being, and contribute to the enduring cultural identity and the visual harmony of communities.

Understanding the Risks

> "Don't ask what will happen. Be what happens."
> —Rebecca Solnit, writer, historian, and activist

A 2018 report by the United Nations Intergovernmental Panel on Climate Change (IPCC) stated that just half a degree of additional warming could make the difference between whether flooding will impact up to sixty-nine million people or as many as eighty million people by the year 2100. In the South, we are concerned with hurricanes, tornadoes, floods, extreme precipitation events, and the occasional earthquake. So, it's important to understand the risks when planning to build.

This includes environmental risks, which are also important to ascertain when buying property. The noise and electrical waves from Bitcoin farms and the chemicals, stink, and toxic runoff from paper mills and pig farms—these are all causes for concern because they will affect the health and well-being of residents in the neighborhood. Always check the zoning laws to ensure that your property won't be next to an eyesore or health hazard.

RESOURCES

- Climate Change Assessment Southeast, https://nca2018.globalchange.gov/chapter/19/
- FEMA National Risk Index, https://hazards.fema.gov/nri/
- Flood Risk Factors, https://riskfactor.com/
- NOAA Sea Level Rise, https://coast.noaa.gov/slr/#

Designing for Your Risks

Historically, we have worried more about hurricanes with high winds, but in 2018 Hurricane Florence proved that Category 1 storms can be just as disastrous. In South Carolina, eight people died, there was over $607 million in property damage, and more than two thousand homes were lost to flooding.

The American Society of Heating, Refrigerating, and Air-Conditioning Engineers (ASHRAE) Guide for Buildings in Hot & Humid Climates recommends designing and constructing buildings in hurricane-prone areas by using the following steps, listed in order of priority:

- Keep the building from blowing away
- Keep the rain out
- Elevate the structure above the floodplain
- Build with materials that tolerate soaking
- Design the wall assemblies to dry easily when they become wet

Keep the Building from Blowing Away

A building must be designed with a continuous load path that ensures that all structural elements work together to resist high winds and uplift forces. The roof trusses or rafters are secured to the walls with metal hurricane straps or clips. Likewise, the walls are securely bolted to the foundation. The building also must be designed to withstand lateral forces from winds or seismic activity, which act in a perpendicular fashion against the structural members of a building. The structural engineer will design shear walls or use steel framing to resist these lateral loads. Other important preventive measures include keeping trees trimmed of dead wood, since these can become potential missiles able to strike the house with enough force to cause damage.

Windows and doors should also be protected from flying objects because if the windows or doors (or both) are compromised, the roof can blow off. The simplest way to do this (but not the cheapest) is to install impact-rated windows and doors. Other options include installing hurricane-rated shutters or fitting PVC-coated woven fabric or plywood panels over the openings, fastened as per the building code. The exterior materials should be rated to withstand hurricane-force winds and must be securely installed per the manufacturer's recommendations.

Keep the Rain Out

Keeping rainwater out of the building is fairly straightforward—but only if design decisions are made to address this. (See chapter 4 for a detailed discussion on the building enclosure and keeping rain out of a building.)

Prevent Flood Damage

The next consideration is elevating the building and employing mechanical systems as a way to minimize contact with floodwater and a potential storm surge. It may be prudent to place your house well above the required base flood elevation level due to rising sea levels.

Crawl spaces that are located in a flood hazard zone will need hydrostatic vents to prevent floodwaters from collapsing foundation walls. These hydrostatic vents allow floodwater to enter and exit the crawl space. Finally, use materials that can tolerate soaking and can dry easily.

The steel moment frame is used to resist lateral loads from hurricane-force winds.

Flood Hazard Zones

In many communities, flooding is a major concern. New structures are required to be elevated above the base flood elevation if they are in a flood hazard zone. Base flood elevations are reevaluated periodically, so an older home may actually lie below the revised flood elevation and be subject to FEMA's 50 Percent Rule (see below). Special consideration should be given before buying an existing home where the first floor of livable space is below the base flood elevation. A surveyor will identify the floor elevation in relation to the base flood elevation and can provide an elevation certificate for an existing house to verify that the building is properly elevated. You can also look up your flood hazard zone on the FEMA website.

FLOOD HAZARD ZONES ARE RATED AS FOLLOWS:

- V-Zone (Velocity Zone): Coastal high hazard subject to 100-year flooding and storm surge
- A-Zones: High risk of flooding
- B-Zone and X-Zone shaded: Moderate risk of flooding
- C-Zone and X-Zone unshaded: Minimal risk of flooding

FEMA's 50 Percent Rule

According to FEMA's 50 Percent Rule, if the cost of improvements or repair to a damaged building exceeds 50 percent of the building's market value, then the entire building must be brought into compliance with the NFIP requirements. The market value calculation is for the building only, not the property, any landscape improvements, or detached accessory buildings. This value can be determined with the help of a licensed appraiser or a municipality's property assessment.

The only items excluded from the cost of improvements or repair are the following:

- Plans and specification
- Surveys
- Permit fees
- Cost to demolish storm-damaged buildings
- Debris removal
- Landscape improvements
- Detached structures (If the detached structure is a habitable space, it is subject to the same 50 Percent Rule.)

Many existing houses currently in the flood hazard zones do not meet the NFIP requirements; thus, they must adhere to the 50 Percent Rule or raise the building out of the floodplain to meet FEMA's guidelines. Municipalities often adopt a cumulative substantial improvement policy for buildings that combines structural repairs, reconstruction, rehabilitation, additions, or other improvements, during a finite period of time that is limited by the 50 Percent Rule. One municipality may have a five-year cumulative policy while another's is a ten-year policy. Check with your local building department for your municipality's regulations.

Lifting a house sounds like a very big undertaking, but it is a wise move if you have a house that is below the base flood elevation. In a world with rising sea levels and increasingly severe weather, flooding is a nightmare that will only get more prevalent. A good example of lifting a house to make it more resilient can be found in this chapter's case study, the transformation of a dated beach house on Fripp Island in South Carolina.

Accommodating

Accommodating refers to planning how a home might change in the future to make it more adaptable to climate change and other risks. Accommodation is frequently associated with home renovation projects, as in this chapter's case study. Other accommodating steps might include "soft" or natural protection measures, such as wetlands restoration.

Retreating

The skills and expertise of your architect can help you decide whether to renovate, rebuild, or retreat. Older homes past their prime may require such decisions, since these houses often include resilient and nonresilient design considerations, such as dated kitchens, small nonfunctional bathrooms with ugly tile, little windows overlooking a great view, and rooms built below FEMA's base flood elevation. Perhaps you own one of these properties or are considering buying one for the view. Homeowners of older properties will often reach the point where they have three options:

- Renovate, add an addition to the existing house, or both (This might include raising the house and is the most sustainable option when you consider the amount of construction waste kept out of the landfill.)
- Tear the existing house down and build a new house on the same property
- Move

SHOULD I STAY OR SHOULD I GO?

To help decide whether you should stay or go after your home has incurred storm damage, here are a few questions to consider:

- Do you love the location?
- Do you have a great view?
- Is the house built above FEMA's base flood elevation requirements? If it is below these requirements, then you are limited to spending 50 percent of the value of the house on the renovation. Otherwise, the house has to be raised.
- Is the house built behind the current coastal or municipality setbacks? If your house is in the setback, you cannot add any square footage in the setback, but you can keep what is there, which might be an advantage.
- Will current zoning laws allow additions to your house?
- Will you overbuild for the neighborhood?

Building Above Code

While you will have to build to code, you also should consider building *above* the code. IBHS offers the following example from when 2018's Hurricane Michael came ashore with 160 mph winds.

Paul Jackson of Mexico Beach, Florida, had built his home to comply with the IBHS Fortified Gold standard. During Hurricane Michael, Paul's house survived while his neighbors' didn't. The Florida code requirement for wind design was to withstand up to 140 mph winds, but Jackson's home was designed for 160 mph winds—which made all the difference for his house. Most states adopt and modify the International Residential Code, while other states do not have a statewide code. So it is possible that even if you have been issued a building permit, the home you build could still be in trouble.

Alabama, Georgia, Texas, and Mississippi do not have a statewide building code. In these states, we recommend building to the Florida building code or to the IBHS Fortified Gold standard. These states have the lowest rating from the Insurance Institute for Business & Home Safety (discussed previously): Compare Mississippi's score of 29 to Florida's score of 95.

FORTIFIED HOME

This certification by IBHS is one way of monitoring a home while it's under construction to ensure that it's as resilient as possible. The FORTIFIED Home certification (along with the building codes we are required to design to, whether wind or earthquake) also play into the sustainability and resilience of a home. The program's website explains:

> FORTIFIED is a better way to build, re-roof, or retrofit your home to protect against severe weather. It doesn't take a hurricane or tornado to cause major damage to your home. In fact, storm winds as low as 50 mph can cause damage that allows water to enter your home. FORTIFIED helps you protect against this type of damage by addressing known weaknesses in common building practices (fortifiedhome.org).

All postrenovation photographs in this case study courtesy of John McManus

CASE STUDY: RESILIENCY

Our clients had owned this house for many years, and the entire family had a sentimental attachment to it. However, the home just wasn't big enough for their newly blended family of seven children. As an older home, it also had issues that needed to be remedied.

The house was built in 1976 and had not been updated since. As a result, the interiors felt dark and closed off . . . and very '70s (and not in a cool, vintage way). The first floor was below the base flood elevation in a flood hazard zone. Our mission was to save the house and lift it up out of the floodplain.

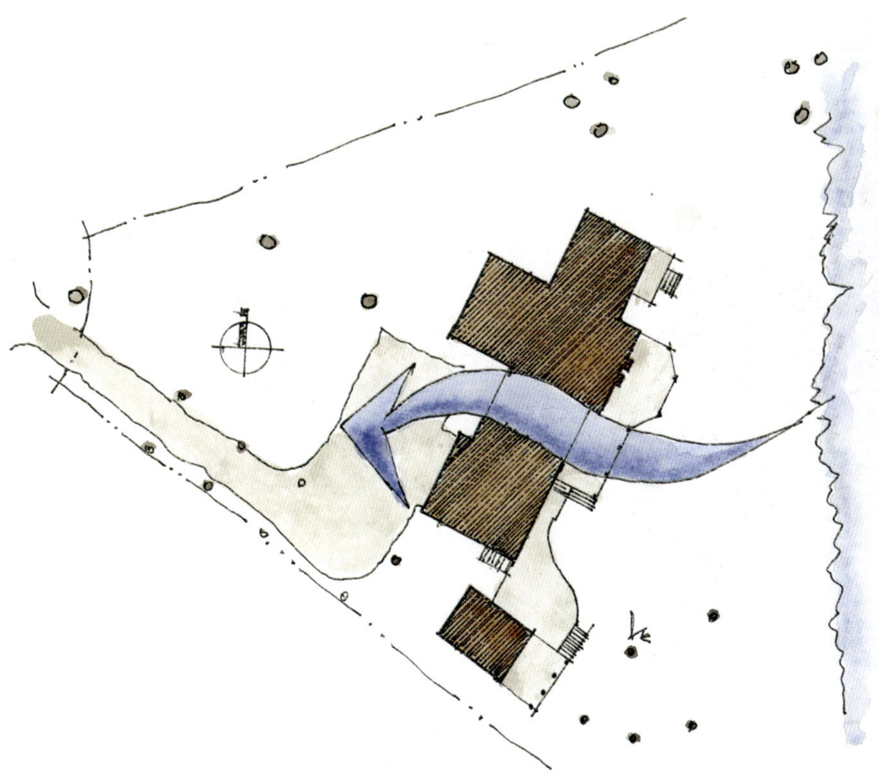

We contacted a national house moving company, one with experience moving and lifting houses along the East Coast. Once the building permit was issued, the contractor prepared the house for the lift by disconnecting the utilities and the existing fasteners that anchored the house to the foundation. After the electricity was disconnected, a new temporary power pole was installed. The chimney was also removed. Then the house movers lifted the house, using hydraulic jacks, and rested it on temporary cribbing.

ABOVE: The rear of the house before the renovation

RIGHT: The house is supported on temporary cribbing while the new foundation is built.

LEFT: The front exterior before the renovation

BELOW: The front exterior after the renovation

The contractor then built a new foundation underneath the lifted home. After this was complete, the movers returned and lowered the house down onto its new foundation. We were able to save the whole house just by raising it 4 feet, so it was now 2 feet above the base flood elevation. The expense of the lift was a fraction of what it would have cost to demolish the house and build a completely new one—plus this prevented tons of debris from being taken to the landfill.

RIGHT: The kitchen before the renovation

Once the house was safely raised, it was then renovated to meet the current code. The interior walls were taken down to the studs. New mechanical, electrical, and plumbing systems were added, and building enclosure upgrades were made. Plus new insulation was added, making the house far more energy efficient than it was before.

ABOVE LEFT: The living room before the renovation

Resiliency: Sustainable Strategies

VERNACULAR

- Existing house renovated

CONTEMPORARY

- Raised the house above the base flood elevation
- New efficient HVAC system
- New WaterSense faucets and fixtures
- Impact windows and doors with high-performance glass
- VOC-free paint
- Tight building enclosure
- Secondary roof

Project Completed: 2018

Builder: A & D Homebuilders
Beaufort, South Carolina

Courtesy of Jeff Amberg

CHAPTER 8
A Joy Forever

"There is nothing like staying home for real comfort."
—Eleanor Roosevelt

We have presented a lot of information about how to build a sustainable, resilient home—which can seem complicated. Some of the means and methods we describe might be new to your builder, so it is essential to have the construction and systems verified before completing the build of your home.

In this chapter, we will cover different aspects of how to make sure your home is a joy forever. This includes the construction verification, understanding the importance of commissioning (bringing things into working order) during the operation of your home's systems, and recommendations for ongoing maintenance.

Verification During Construction

It's important to get the necessary verifications while your home is being constructed, because when you're building to strict standards, you want to ensure they have been followed. Architects are instrumental in confirming that a building is assembled in accordance with the construction documents. This proactive step ensures that your home is not only aesthetically pleasing but also structurally sound and aligned with your design goals.

The architect and engineers will prepare the construction documents, detailing how the house is to be built so that it will meet sustainability and resiliency goals, the desired aesthetic, and the required quality of construction, as well as the building code requirements. Architects are the best people to ascertain that the house is built in accordance with the construction documents, since they are thinking about the project from its inception.

Construction administration includes reviewing and approving the submittal packages of windows, doors, plumbing fixtures, etc. and payment requests, as well as visiting the construction site regularly throughout the build. Often, homeowners think that they can save money by not hiring an architect to provide construction administration; however, even with a complete set of documents, questions will still arise during construction. If an architect isn't there to answer questions, then it is left to the homeowner or builder to answer them. It's difficult for builders to come up with proper solutions without knowing the design intent. Usually the builder will build as they have always done before, neglecting details such as the air, water, and thermal control layers needed to create the tight building enclosure.

An architect friend, Jakie, told us how he was once commissioned to design a house in the mountains—but he wasn't hired for the construction administration. When the structure was almost completely built, Jakie visited the house. He looked and looked and finally told the builder, "This doesn't look anything like the drawings." The builder replied, "Well, you have to admit, it kinda resembles them." Your investment is too big to have your home "kinda resemble" your architect's drawings.

Here's another example of when integral architect verification is required. We've encountered shear walls that were designed with specific nailing requirements to meet the lateral loads for hurricanes or earthquakes. Yet, these are frequently left unchecked by building inspectors, leaving it uncertain whether the shear walls were installed as required by the structural engineer's design. When an architect is on-site for construction administration, they will ensure the correct construction of the wall.

Architects are the owner's representative during construction, and they work in concert with the builder. The most valuable activities they provide are problem-solving and observing the construction during regular visits to the jobsite. During these visits, they can observe whether the project is being built in

A jobsite meeting with the architect and contractors

accordance with the construction documents and can answer any questions that the builder or subcontractors might have.

At our practice, we partner with the builder to figure out the best solutions. We document site visits with a field report that states who was on-site, how far along the project was, what we discussed, what issues arose during construction, and any changes required. We also attach sketches that might be needed to clarify the discussions, as well as photographs of the work in progress.

Architects will protect your interests during construction administration by making sure that best practices are followed. For example, in a humid climate, it is advantageous to have the house conditioned when interior finishes are being installed (*see image at right*). Wood has a high moisture content during installation. If this practice of conditioning the air during the interior finish installation isn't followed, when the air-conditioning is turned on later, the wood will dry and shrink, compromising all the joints.

One best practice is to require temporary heating and cooling once the roof, walls, doors, and windows are installed and it is dry inside the building. At this point, the electrical, mechanical, and plumbing systems are installed. Conditioning in this way is accomplished by placing a portable HVAC unit outside, with ducts going into the window, as opposed to using the permanent system. Imagine if all the construction dust was in your expensive HVAC unit and ducts.

One independent test that must be performed during construction, which we touched on in chapter 4, is the blower door test. This test identifies any compromises in the air control layer of the building enclosure. Ideally, you will perform the blower door test twice: once after the mechanical, electrical, and plumbing rough-ins are installed and before insulation, then again at the end of construction, to make sure the air control layer wasn't compromised during the rest of construction. If the control layers in the building enclosure have holes in them, water can seep in, allowing moisture to cause mold issues.

Insurance Institute for Business & Home Safety's FORTIFIED Home

Earning an independent certification for the building, such as FORTIFIED Home, not only creates a stronger home but also has potential financial benefits for the home insurer and may result in tax credits (depending on location). State-specific financial incentives are outlined on IBHS's website.

We are FORTIFIED Home–certified professionals, and we receive weekly calls from owners wanting to get their home certified. Unfortunately, most of the calls come after the project completion; the certification process must occur during construction. One caller, an insurance agent, told us that if the house was Gold certified, it would have saved his client $5,000 annually.

Employing a temporary HVAC system protects the permanent system from construction dust.

The certification program includes three levels of upgrades to protect a home from severe weather: Fortified Roof, Silver, or Gold. These design standards are based on decades of research and require upgrades to the roof and building.

FORTIFIED ROOF

The IBHS FORTIFIED Home identifies the roof as the most important component in protecting your house. FORTIFIED Roof is applicable both to new construction and to existing buildings when the roof is replaced. Certification requires specific detailing for a stronger roof edge, a sealed roof deck, better attachments, and impact-resistant shingles, tiles, or metal roofing.

SILVER STANDARD

The Silver level builds on the FORTIFIED Roof level by certifying that all exterior doors, windows, and garage doors are pressure- and impact-rated or protected with a qualified system, such as shutters. The Silver level also requires that attached porches and carports be properly connected to prevent uplift during high winds, as well as requiring chimney bracing and gable end bracing.

GOLD STANDARD

This is the most advanced level of certification, and it includes everything in both the FORTIFIED Roof and Silver levels, with the addition of engineer-designed connections that tie the roof rafters to the walls, the walls to the floor, and the floor to the foundation. It also includes stronger exterior sheathing. The requirements for the Silver and Gold standards mean that they are achievable only during a major renovation or new construction.

The FORTIFIED Home certification is good for five years, at which point the home will need to be reinspected. Before too long, we think that insurance companies will also be requiring the FORTIFIED Home certification as a requirement for insurance in hurricane-prone areas.

LEED Certification for Homes, Living Building Challenge, and EarthCraft

LEED Certification for Homes, Living Building Challenge, and EarthCraft are some third-party programs dedicated to sustainable housing. LEED Certification for Homes is a program that recognizes sustainable design and construction practices, ensuring energy efficiency, water conservation, and environmental responsibility. Living Building Challenge is a rigorous sustainability standard promoting regenerative design, requiring net-zero energy, water, and waste, among others. EarthCraft is a green building certification program focused on energy efficiency, indoor air quality, and sustainability for residential and commercial buildings.

Each includes point-based systems with stringent criteria to promote energy efficiency, resource conservation, and environmental responsibility. These green building certifications also prioritize health, resilience, and reduced environmental impact. Through rigorous assessments, the programs establish benchmarks to guide the creation of healthier, more sustainable living spaces.

Operations and Commissioning Systems

Once your sustainable, resilient home is complete, you need to ensure that it maintains its high-performance, healthy, and resilient condition. This entails commissioning to make sure that the systems—mechanical, electrical, and plumbing—are working correctly, education about operating the high-performance systems, and the need to perform ongoing maintenance. Commissioning the mechanical systems is a way of testing them to determine that the systems function as designed. The installation contractor will also explain how to operate and maintain the systems.

MECHANICAL

Homeowners need to understand the advantages and limitations of their mechanical systems, especially when it comes to heat pumps. Heat pumps do not generate heat; they only exchange heat from the outside to the inside. Many people who come to the South from colder climates are used to furnaces to heat their home, so they may expect a blast of hot air when raising the thermostat.

We once had a client who would turn the heat in her guesthouse down to 55 degrees at night, then crank it up in the morning when she used the space to practice yoga. She was convinced that the system didn't work; it did, just not in the way she wanted it to. In a house with heat pumps, it's important to change the temperature on the thermostat only a few degrees when in heat mode. If the temperature change is too great, the unit will use the backup heat strip to warm the space, and this is inefficient and costly. When operating a heat pump in a hot, humid climate, set the fan to "auto." When it is set to "fan only," the fan will run continuously rather than cycling as it should to remove humidity from the air, which can cause air quality and potential mold issues.

ELECTRICAL

Home energy management systems (HEMS) can be installed into the home during construction. This system will tell you the exact amount of energy each circuit draws. If the circuit starts to draw more energy than usual, then you know there is a problem and where that problem occurs. Research by Lockheed Martin Energy for the New York State Energy Research and Development Authority found that while whole-house energy monitors saved money, an easier and less expensive solution was to use smart thermostats, outlets, and lights. Smart products produced an annual energy reduction of 16 percent, more than the average 10 percent reduction with a HEMS.

PLUMBING

The Insurance Information Institute reports that around 20 percent of homeowner insurance claims are due to water damage (excluding flooding). Water damage losses range in the billions of dollars every year. Fortunately, leak detectors are easy and inexpensive to install. Be sure to install a whole-house leak detector while the home is still under construction. If a leak is discovered, there is a shutoff valve; if you are out of town and your water heater bursts, the detector will close the valve so your whole house doesn't flood.

Maintenance

When you buy a new automobile, you receive a regular maintenance schedule that instructs you to bring your car to the auto shop and have different services performed at different times—at 5,000 miles, at 10,000 miles, and so on. People seem to understand and accept this when it comes to cars. However, when it comes to maintaining your home, most people sort of wing it. And it's not hard to understand why. When home construction is complete, the homeowners aren't handed that same kind of service schedule.

Now that you have built your resilient, highly efficient, and sustainable home, regular maintenance is crucial. Your house is probably one of the biggest investments that you'll ever make. Learning how to operate and maintain it might feel complicated, with all its different systems and low-maintenance materials, but low maintenance is not no maintenance, especially in hot, humid climates.

Every resilient, sustainable home is unique and requires a detailed user's manual. This manual should include everything you will need to maintain your home: the model numbers and operational manuals for all the system components and appliances; the names and contact information of the subcontractors who installed the systems; the size of your filters and location; paint colors; warranty documents for building components such as doors, windows, and mechanical systems; and the recommended maintenance and service schedule. Over the years, update this manual as appliances and systems are replaced. Maintaining these maintenance records will be an asset when the house is sold.

GENERAL MAINTENANCE AND SERVICE CALENDAR

We have created a general maintenance and service calendar (specific to the seasons) that can be customized for your house. This list does not include the regular general cleaning of your house, which is typically done weekly or biweekly or on an as-needed basis.

Monthly

- Check all the filters in your house monthly and change them if needed. This includes water purification filters in your ice maker, HVAC filters, and ERV filters.
- Clean range hood filters and dishwasher filters. Most range hood filters can be run through the dishwasher.

Spring

Spring is a great time for general maintenance in preparation for the high winds and heavy rains of the upcoming hurricane season, which starts in June.

- Clean the gutters and downspouts and make sure the downspouts direct the water away from the house.
- Inspect the roof and make sure it is in good shape. Be sure to blow off any leaf debris.
- Every few years, remove the deadwood from large trees to prevent damage from branches in a storm.
- Test your smoke and carbon monoxide alarms. Replace the batteries when you change the clocks for daylight saving time.

Some exterior maintenance items should wait until after the live oak leaves have fallen and the heavy pollen days have passed. These include the following:

- Power-wash the house and paving to remove mold and mildew.
- Wash the windows.
- Clean the photovoltaic panels.
- Make sure that leaves have not built up around the exterior HVAC unit.

A few maintenance items should be contracted with a local company, such as a bond with a termite company.

- Schedule an annual inspection for termites before they start swarming.
- Contact your HVAC company for spring and fall maintenance prior to the heavy cooling and heating seasons.

Fall

Many of the spring maintenance items repeat in the fall.

- Clean the gutters.
- Power-wash the terraces and walks.
- Have the HVAC system serviced.
- If the home has a chimney, have it cleaned by a chimney sweep, especially if you have a woodburning fireplace.

Annually

Several items should be inspected annually to see if they warrant attention.

- Inspect exterior paint
- Reseal stone countertops
- Replace the anode rod in the water heater. The anode rod is a sacrificial component in electric water heaters that attracts corrosion and mineral buildup, which protects the other metals. By replacing the corroded anode rod, the life of the electric water heater will be extended by years.

Minimize Landscaping Maintenance

As discussed in chapter 3, when you use native plants and minimize the amount of lawn, the yard becomes low maintenance because it requires less water and fertilizer to keep plants healthy. Other benefits of native landscaping include the following:

- Deer will not eat the plants.
- Birds and animals will thrive on the native plants when there is not a monoculture of grass.
- Oak leaves provide excellent mulch for camellias and azaleas.
- Composting kitchen vegetable scraps will also provide excellent natural mulch.

Case Study: Low Maintenance

The client's request was for a light-filled house where a Stickley sofa would look at home. Our concept was to draw inspiration from Stickley's design principles of handicraft married with a modern functional simplicity to create a home with open floor plans, economy of function, and a biophilic material palette. To meet the AIA's 2030 Commitment goals, we turned to the local vernacular form of the T-house, with the longest leg running east west. This allowed all rooms to have windows on both sides for light and cross ventilation. The use of a 10.5 kW photovoltaic array reduced the predicted energy use by 70 percent.

The T-plan, with its single-room width and elongated form, is slanted on the lot to frame an extensive view of a monumental live oak to the east. Craftsman-era elements, such as exposed rafters, a low-pitched roof, and inclined entry columns, are reinterpreted in a contemporary style.

A long kitchen cabinet wall transitions into a Craftsman-style fireplace that incorporates modern geometry. The shed roofs slope to the south and open to the northern light and views of the pond and large live oaks. There is an extensive rain garden on the entry side with native plants that filter roof runoff and create an exciting entry sequence.

The interior finishes and color palette were selected to harmonize with and evoke nature. The Skyfall granite island countertop ties together the oak cabinets and handmade celadon backsplash tiles. The abstract pattern of the fireplace tile is reminiscent of the surface of the pond. Leaf-shaped tiles were selected for the master shower.

The house was designed to incorporate a number of high-performance systems. The HVAC system was designed in-house to be the most efficient and appropriately sized system for the house and the client.

The clients had not considered installing a photovoltaic array when they started the process of envisioning their new house. We presented them with a detailed return on investment for solar, including an analysis of state and federal tax credits available. This information and the fact that they could eliminate the need for an emergency generator by adding a 14 kW Tesla Powerwall battery proved that renewable energy with storage capacity was a sound financial decision.

Low Maintenance: Sustainable Strategies

VERNACULAR

- T-house form with the longest leg running east–west
- Placement of the home on the site to take advantage of sun angles and prevailing breezes
- Single-width rooms for cross ventilation
- High ceilings
- Large overhangs

CONTEMPORARY

- High-efficiency home
- High-efficiency heat pumps with an ERV
- Solar panels
- Battery backup
- Energy Star LED lighting
- Low-SHGC glass
- Blower door test
- VOC-free paint
- WaterSense plumbing fixtures

Project Completed: 2019

Contractor: Esposito Construction Hilton Head Island, South Carolina

Landscape Architect: Verdant Enterprises, Savannah, Georgia

CHAPTER 9
Aging in Place

"Home is not just a place; it's a feeling of comfort, safety, and belonging."

—Rick Bragg, *All Over but the Shoutin'*

"According to the AARP in 2021, if given the choice, 77 percent of adults over 50 would prefer to age in place. This personal preference is reflected in the data: in the past 20 years, the number of community-dwelling adults in traditional housing has increased, while those living in nursing homes has declined, and in 2020 only 1.2 million adults over 65 were nursing home residents."

—National Library of Medicine, "Aging in Place," 2021

Socially, older adults derive comfort and identity from remaining connected to neighborhoods and communities they have known for years. Often, older relatives will be happier staying in a multigenerational home, because it fosters interactions between grandparents and grandchildren. Lifelong memories and emotional attachments make a home more than just shelter—it becomes an integral part of your personal story. Ideally, your home will reflect your stage in life. Architects can anticipate your future needs in order to design a home where the layout can be adapted for different uses as families grow and change.

There are as many situations where a home's layout can be adapted as there are changing needs for homeowners. For example, as we touched on earlier in the book, when babies are part of the family, you might want an area off your primary bedroom for a crib. Whereas, once the children have grown, you can turn that nursery space into a sitting area. A guesthouse can become a place where a caregiver can live, if needed. A primary bedroom on the main floor can be used as a guest suite when kids are little, and then, once they are older, parents can move downstairs, giving themselves and their children a little more privacy.

The use of your house often changes significantly before and after retirement. Before you retire, you share the house after work, often in joint activities. Once you retire and are home more of the day, the need for individual retreats is important. Spare bedrooms can do double duty as exercise rooms, offices, or hobby rooms.

The NCOA (National Council on Aging) conducted a recent study titled "Aging in Place in America," which found that the majority of older adults prefer to age in place and remain in their own homes for as long as possible. The study also highlighted the benefits of aging in place, which included an improved quality of life, a greater sense of independence, and better mental and emotional well-being.

When Jane's mom, Ann, was diagnosed with dementia, we made some changes to our home so she could live with us. We remodeled our daughters' bedrooms into a suite with a bedroom and sitting room with a kitchenette. We even painted the walls and installed tile in the same colors she had at her house, to make it an easy transition from her home of fifty years.

Successfully aging in place requires forethought and planning. In this chapter, we will explore some of the opportunities and challenges of aging in place and provide tips for how you can proactively plan for a home that will truly be a joy forever in service of your family and loved ones as they age.

As the global population rapidly ages, aging in place has become an increasingly important concept in architecture, design, policymaking, and community planning. The State of World Population report by the United Nations says that the number of people age sixty years or older doubled from 1980 to 2017, and that by 2050 the number of people over sixty will more than double again, to 2.1 billion. With improved healthcare extending life spans, most adults are living longer. As more baby boomers cross into their retirement years, aging in place will become a increasingly crucial consideration in home design, construction, and community development.

Improved Quality of Life

There are three major areas of consideration for aging in place: life safety, fall prevention, and convenience. When properly designed, homes can support mobility, reduce fall risks, and accommodate changing physical and cognitive abilities. Thoughtful home design features such as ramps, grab bars, lever-style handles, and nonslip flooring promote safety and accessibility. Universal design principles that benefit people of all ages and abilities can be incorporated from the outset of the design.

Life Safety

In case of fire, a major safety issue is to provide an accessible exit from each bedroom, which is a basic building code requirement. The minimum code requirement is a window large enough and low enough to the floor to crawl through. As we age, or if we use a wheelchair or walker, crawling through a window is almost impossible. Therefore, we like to include exterior doors from the primary bedrooms in our home designs, either to a terrace or—in the case of a two-story home—to a balcony or second story porch.

In two-story houses and houses raised up out of the floodplain, we often install a residential elevator or stack elevator-sized closets for a future elevator. When planning for a future elevator, the closet floor should be framed for easy removal, providing the space necessary for the installation of the elevator. In houses less than 5 feet off the ground, we often include a ramp to the back or side door. When thought about during preliminary design, a custom-designed ramp will fit in with the overall architecture of the house.

According to the National Institute of Building Sciences (NIBS), elders are the largest group of wheelchair users. They differ from younger wheelchair users because most of the elders can bear weight and walk short distances but have limited upper-body strength. The elders' issues are gait, balance, strength, and stamina. Ensuring the accessibility of a space for elders often requires allowing space for a companion to walk along with them or assist them in getting on and off the toilet.

Accessible doors are 36 inches wide and preferably have flush thresholds—if not flush, thresholds should be a maximum height of 1/2 inch for exterior doors and 1/4 inch for interior doors. Hallways should be at least 42 inches wide, but 48 inches is preferable because that width can accommodate a wheelchair user or a person walking with an escort, a guide dog, or a walker. Aesthetically, wider halls are a big plus because the home feels more gracious. Every room, including bathrooms, should have an open space of 5 by 5 feet for wheelchair maneuverability. Open floor plans can also improve accessibility.

When you design for accessibility, the components are cohesive, and it doesn't look like an afterthought. For example, several of our clients have had bad backs. For one, we designed a ramp under a covered walkway to take him from the detached garage to the side door of his home. Most of our projects with detached garages have covered walkways to the house, and designing it as a ramp is a pleasing aesthetic.

Another client with a bad back lives on the beach. We included an elevator from the garage, located underneath the house, up to the third floor. Additionally, we built a ramp from the main living floor down to the beach so she could get to the beach without having to take the stairs over the dunes.

ABOVE: Wide halls with plenty of light are essential in accessible homes. *Courtesy of John McManus*

Fall Prevention

Floor material, lighting, and grab bars are the keys to help prevent falls. Floors should be smooth, firm, and slip resistant. Carpet should feature a low pile (less than 1/2 inch) with a firm pad.

There should be plenty of natural light as well as both overall room lighting and task lighting. Proper lighting reduces the risk of falls and aids failing vision. Particular care should be given to lighting stairwells, showers, entry doors, and exterior walkways. Stairwells should have switches at both the top and bottom, and hallways should have them located at both ends. Stairwells should also have handrails on both sides of the stairs. Blocking can be installed in the hallways for future grab bars.

Glare, low contrast, and low illuminance levels are the most common visual impediments in buildings. Careful window placement is important in reducing glare. Shiny finishes also contribute to glare, so honed countertops and a matte finish on tile are preferable. Providing contrasting colors such as a dark floor and light walls or dark hardware on light cabinets and doors helps people with limited vision. Installing curbless showers helps prevent falls in the bathroom and provides easy access for someone with mobility restrictions. We typically put grab bars in showers and bathtubs, as well as blocking for future installation of grab bars around the toilet.

Convenience

Even if their house has an elevator, many of our clients who are close to retirement age want their bedroom on the main floor because of the ease that comes with single-story living. Low-maintenance materials make it easier for people who are getting on in years to care for their home. Other considerations to improve convenience include lever door handles and faucets, which help arthritic hands open doors and work faucets in the kitchen and bathroom.

Smart home technology can also provide the conveniences needed while aging in place. Voice-controlled lights, small appliances, and locks are helpful, as are doors that can be opened by motion sensors or remote control. Technologies can also provide security, reminders for medications, and alert systems in case of emergencies.

Including a separate guesthouse or two master suites can accommodate an aging relative or a live-in caretaker. Having the older generation move into a guesthouse and the younger generation move into the main house is another interesting way that people can age in place in their home. The National Aging in Place Council provides excellent resources for homeowners looking to find out additional information about how they can adapt their home to meet their needs as they age.

Adaptable Layouts

When we consider the life of a home, we sometimes need to change the design to reflect the intention of new homeowners. In 2000, we designed a vacation house for clients who enjoyed hosting visits from a foursome of golfers, creating a layout for a two-bedroom guesthouse with separate entrances. When new clients bought the home, we adapted the layout to make it into a home for their entire family to visit with their children and grandchildren, providing space for everyone to gather and enjoy. We remodeled the two individual suites into a shared guesthouse and added a sitting area. As custom home specialists, we have not had too many repeat clients, but over our thirty-five years, we have had many repeat houses. A lot of the design process is about making the house the client's own.

Courtesy of Kim Smith

Courtesy of Kim Smith

CASE STUDY: LIFE OF A HOUSE

This house is close to our hearts. The Frederick + Frederick–designed residence was built in 2001 as a vacation spot to house a foursome for golf. The current owners hired us to design an addition as well as multiple remodeling projects, including a guesthouse remodel, the addition of a music studio, a new kitchen, a pantry, a powder room, and exterior changes.

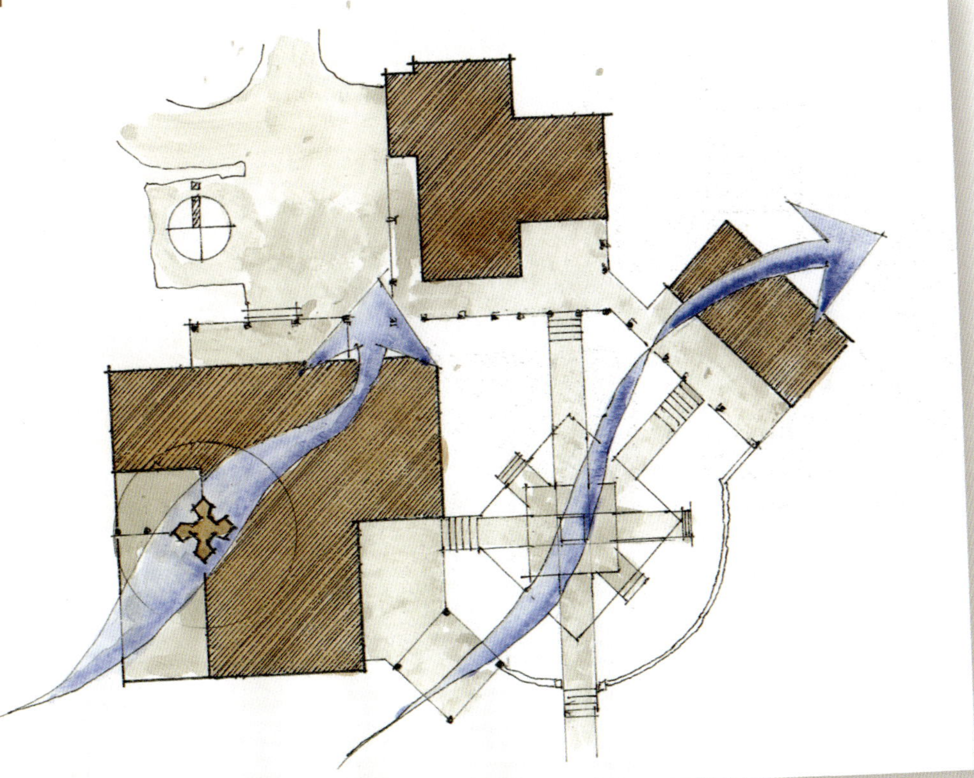

One of the current clients had a simple request: He wanted a place to play his guitars and a room to store them. When discussing the clients' desires, we decided to build a new studio to house the clients' hobbies of playing guitar and quilting and to create a courtyard protected from nibbling deer and creepy-crawlies. The form of the studio building is based on the traditional freedman's cottage.

Photographs courtesy of John McManus

By engaging the senses in the design of the studio, the simple activity of playing guitar becomes a sensuous, impactful experience. The long view of the Shrimp Pond is peaceful and relaxing. The smoothness of the live-edge walnut desk begs to be touched. The aroma of the cypress walls evokes a pleasant walk in the woods as the guitar plays amid great acoustics.

The original guesthouse was designed for hosting a foursome of golfers and had two separate suites connected by an outdoor staircase. We moved the stairs inside and added another bedroom to create a sitting room and media center downstairs. The new studio was positioned on the lot adjacent to the guesthouse to take advantage of the view of the Shrimp Pond.

The interiors of the house, guesthouse, and studio are clad in sinker cypress, which was pulled from the swamps and tributaries of the Apalachicola River in Florida. The tannins in the water alter the colors of the wood from red to brown and from gray or purple to almost black. Once surfaced and finished, the wood practically glows. The cabinets, shoji doors, and several pieces of furniture were designed by the firm and built by a local cabinet-maker. All materials were constructed from this cypress. Live-edge walnut slabs were used for the desktops and vanity. The interiors contain a mixture of new and old pieces of furniture; some of the existing pieces were repurposed, reupholstered, or refinished.

The giant shoji doors (5 feet wide by 10 feet tall) divide the sewing studio from the guitar studio and stack on top of each other when open. We used the same method for the closet doors in the space. This effect creates a rhythm of light and shadow that changes throughout the day.

Courtesy of
John McManus

The kitchen was updated with a new layout, as well as new cabinets and appliances, all to bring more lightness to the space. We also removed some of the exterior porches to increase the connection with the trees and the sky beyond the great room. After living in the house for a while, the owners knew they could eliminate some of the porches that were used less frequently.

Courtesy of Kim Smith

The interior spaces are uniquely built for the homeowners, with three distinctive areas within the great room: a space for morning coffee and birdwatching, an area with a table for cards or intimate meals, and another spot for socializing by the fireplace.

Photographs courtesy of Kim Smith

The new, custom kitchen cabinets were made of structured panels for a streamlined contemporary look and laid out in a way that makes them accessible while maximizing their usefulness. Most of the kitchen storage was moved to the pantry, which was designed to have space for baking, coffee, and a bar. The dog has his spot too—the bench under the window is for him to watch who's coming and going.

Photographs courtesy of Kim Smith

Photographs courtesy of Kim Smith

Life of a House: Sustainable Strategies

VERNACULAR

- Guitar studio based on freedman's cottage
- Placement of the home on the site to take advantage of sun angles and prevailing breezes
- Single-width rooms for cross ventilation
- High ceilings
- Large overhangs
- Exterior circulation

CONTEMPORARY

- High-efficiency home
- High-efficiency heat pumps with an ERV
- Energy Star LED lighting
- Low-SHGC glass
- Blower door test
- VOC-free paint
- WaterSense plumbing fixtures
- River-recovered cypress and pine

Original Project Completed: 2003

Contractor: Seaside Construction Beaufort, South Carolina

Additions & Renovations: 2004, 2018

Contractor: Phifer Contracting Services Beaufort, South Carolina

Landscape Architect: Alan Glassberg, Ridgeland, South Carolina

Courtesy of John McManus

RESOURCES AND REFERENCES

History

Bragg, Rick. *My Southern Journey: True Stories from the Heart of the South*. Columbia, SC: Liberty Street, 2015.

Edgar, Walter. *South Carolina: A History*. Columbia: University of South Carolina Press, 1989.

Haase, Ronald. *Classic Cracker*. Sarasota, FL: Pineapple, 1992.

Hubka, Thomas. "Just Folks Designing: Vernacular Designers and the Generation of Form." In *Common Places: Readings in American Vernacular Architecture*, edited by Dell Upton and John Michael Vlach. Athens: University of Georgia Press, 1986.

Joseph, J. W., ed. *Another's Country: Archaeological and Historical Perspectives on Cultural Interactions in the Southern Colonies*. Tuscaloosa: University of Alabama Press, 2002.

Lane, Mills. *Architecture of the Old South: Georgia*. Savannah, GA: Beehive, 1986.

Lane, Mills. *Architecture of the Old South: Louisiana*. Savannah, GA: Beehive, 1990.

Lane, Mills. *Architecture of the Old South: Mississippi & Alabama*. Savannah, GA: Beehive, 1989.

Lane, Mills. *Architecture of the Old South: South Carolina*. Savannah, GA: Beehive, 1984.

Olmsted, Frederick Law. *The Cotton Kingdom*. New York: Da Capo, 1996.

Rowland, Lawrence S., Alexander Moore, and George C. Rogers. *The History of Beaufort County, South Carolina: 1514–1861*. Columbia: University of South Carolina Press, 1996.

Rowland, Lawrence S., and Stephen R. Wise. *Bridging the Sea Island's Past and Present, 1893–2006: The History of Beaufort County, South Carolina*. Columbia: University of South Carolina Press, 2015.

Rowland, Lawrence S., Stephen Wise, and Gerhard Spieler. *Rebellion, Reconstruction, and Redemption, 1861–1893: The History of Beaufort County, South Carolina*. Columbia: University of South Carolina Press, 2015.

General Home Design

Jacobson, Max, Murray Silverstein, and Barbara Winslow. *Patterns of Home: The Ten Essentials of Enduring Design*. Newtown, CT: Taunton, 2005.

Lynch, Kevin, and Gary Hack. *Site Planning*. Cambridge, MA: MIT Press, 2002.

Moor, Lisandra. "Japanese Words We Can't Translate—the Essence of Japanese Garden Design." https://www. tokyoweekender.com.

Building Science & Sustainability

Bailes, Allison A. *A House Needs to Breathe . . . or Does It? An Introduction to Building Science*. Hellertown, PA: Bright Communications, 2022.

"BuildingGreen." BuildingGreen. https://buildinggreen.com/.

Clark, Melissa. "The Case for Induction Cooking, versus Gas Stoves." *New York Times*, March 11, 2022.

Cook, Miki, and Doug Garrett. *Green Home Building*. Gabriola Island, BC: New Society, 2014.

Cotrone, Vincent. "The Role of Trees and Forests in Healthy Watersheds." https://extension.psu.edu.

"Declare." International Living Future Institute. https://declare.living-future.org.

EarthCraft. https://www.earthcraft.org.

Energy Star. https://www.energystar.gov/.

Hawken, Paul, ed. *Drawdown*. New York: Penguin, 2017.

Hosey, Lance. *The Shape of Green: Aesthetic, Ecology and Design*. Washington, DC: Island, 2012.

Hyde, Richard. *Climate Responsive Design*. Suffolk, UK: St. Edmundsbury, 2000.

Kennicott, Phillip. "Addicted to Cool." *Washington Post*, September 21, 2023.

Kolbert, Dan, Emily Mottram, Michael Maines, and Christopher Briley. *Pretty Good House: A Guide to Creating Better Homes*. Newtown, CT: Taunton, 2022.

LEED Certification for Homes. https://www.usgbc.org/leed/rating-systems/residential.

Lstiburek, Joe. *Builder's Guide: Hot Humid Climates.* Somerville, MA: Building Science Press, 2005.

Mazria, Ed. "Architects Pollute!" *Metropolis*, October 2003.

McHarg, Ian L. *Design with Nature.* New York: Wiley, 1992.

Squire, Corey. *People, Planet, Design: A Practical Guide to Realizing Architecture's Potential.* Washington, DC: Island, 2023.

Venolia, Carol, and Kelly Lerner. *Natural Remodeling for the Not-So-Green House.* New York: Lark Books, 2006.

Visram, Talib. "Low-Income Neighborhoods Have Fewer Trees. Here's Why That's a Problem." *Fast Company*, June 2021.

Biophilia

Kellert, Stephen R., Judith H. Heerwagen, and Martin L. Mador, eds. *Biophilic Design.* Hoboken, NJ: Wiley, 2008.

Louv, Richard. *Last Child in the Woods.* Chapel Hill, NC: Algonquin Books, 2005.

Wilson, Alex. "Biophilia in Practice: Buildings that Connect People with Nature." https://buildinggreen.com.

Wilson, Edward O. *Biophilia.* Cambridge, MA: Harvard University Press, 1984.

Materials

Baker-Laporte, Paula, and John Banta. *Prescriptions for a Healthy House: A Practical Guide for Architects, Builders and Homeowners.* 4th ed. BLB Publications, 2022.

Cradle to Cradle. https://c2ccertified.org/.

GREENGUARD. https://www.ul.com/services/ul-greenguard-certification.

Grossman, Elizabeth. "Banned in Europe, Safe in the US." https://ensia.com.

"Mindful Materials." Mindful MATERIALS. https://www.mindfulmaterials.com/.

Origin Build. https://origin.build/#/.

The Red List. https://living-future.org/red-list/.

Spot. https://spot.ul.com/.

Resiliency

Community Resilience Planning Guide. https://www.nist.gov/community-resilience/planning-guide.

FEMA Flood Hazard Zones. https://msc.fema.gov/portal/home.

IBHS Fortified Home. https://fortifiedhome.org/.

IBHS Fortified Home Financial Incentives. https://fortifiedhome.org/incentives/.

Aging in Place

The National Aging in Place Council. https://www.naipc.org.

INDEX

ABOUT THE AUTHORS

Jane and Michael Frederick have run their architectural firm, Frederick + Frederick Architects in Beaufort, South Carolina, for more than thirty-five years, focusing exclusively on how the Southern vernacular traditions can merge with the latest technology for optimal building in hot, humid climates. They've won numerous awards for their residential designs and have been featured in the *Wall Street Journal*, *Southern Living*, *Garden & Gun*, and *This Old House*, among many other media outlets.

Jane Frederick, FAIA, was the 2020 president of the American Institute of Architects (AIA). In 2023, Jane was awarded the AIA South Carolina Medal of Distinction, the highest award given by the chapter. Jane holds a bachelor of architecture from Auburn University and is a LEED-accredited professional. She is also a fellow of the Aspen Global Leadership Network. She has been featured in *Madam Architect* and has written extensively on sustainability, resiliency, and building in hot, humid climates in such publications as *Architect*, the *Statehouse Report*, the *Beaufort Gazette*, and *South Carolina Architecture*. Jane is also an international speaker and has been a keynote speaker at the AIA conferences.

Michael Frederick designs AIA award-winning custom residences that provide lasting value and truly celebrate the region's architectural and natural heritage. Knowledge of historical and vernacular architecture coupled with a keen ability to combine timeless architectural truths with current advancements ensures Michael's designs always exceed client expectations. Michael holds a bachelor of architecture from Auburn University. He is a member of the AIA and is both an LEED-accredited professional and a Living Future–accredited professional.